Happy reading!

[illegible]

A

LIGHT ON MAIN STREET©

Written and published by Rudy Taylor

2006

Printed in the United States of America

For information:
Rudy Taylor
P.O. Box 186
Caney, KS 67333

Visit *rudytaylorbooks.com*

Library of Congress Cataloging-in-Publication Data
Taylor, Rudy
Light On Main Street: Storytelling by a Country Newspaper Editor
ISBN 0-9785559-0-2

Printed and Bound by
Central Plains Books, Winfield, Kansas

The possibilities you see
as you peer out life's window
make each ray of light an opportunity for joy.

Rudy Taylor

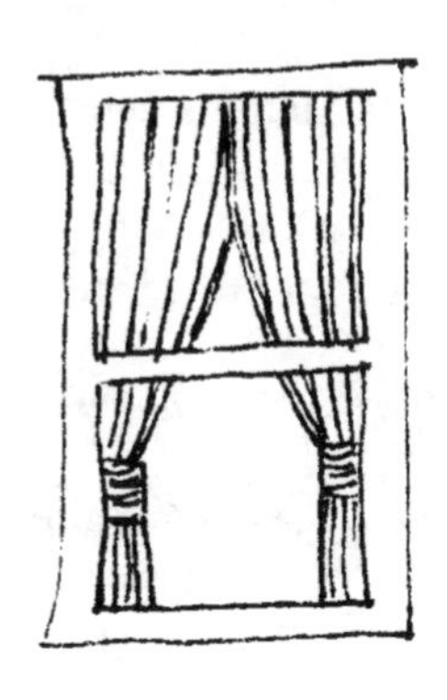

Dedication

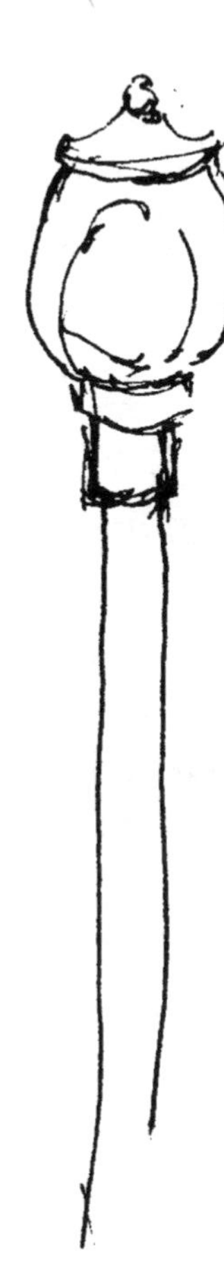

This book is dedicated to Clarence the angel. Because of his or her frequent appearances in my life, I know that everyone has a purpose, and just being born and allowed to live in this wonderful world was a gift from the Almighty ... to all of us.

Forward

By Bill Kurtis

Prairie beauty.

You find it in all colors, shapes and perspectives as you drive across the rolling Flint Hills of Kansas. It is a cluster of osage orange trees in the middle of a lush, green pasture. It is the quiet, warm winds that waft across a green terrain. It is sandstone outcroppings, so perfectly layered with brownish yellow colors straight from the creator's palette.

The Kansas prairies have risen other forms of beauty, notably its authors, many of them newspaper editors. For more than a century, their words have echoed, not only across their communities or even their home state, but throughout the nation and world, as well. Names like William Allen White, Clyde Reed and Rolla Clymer come to mind. Even humorist Will Rogers from the neighboring state of Oklahoma staked a claim to prairie journalism, his column carried by dozens of Kansas newspapers.

Today, another name resounds in Kansas journalism -- Taylor. And, while nobody in the well-known Taylor Newspaper Family would compare themselves to the likes of the legends mentioned above, they are the very essence of prairie-type writing.

Rudy Taylor probably writes more editorials than the editor of the New York Times writes. He does so because the seven small newspapers published by his family in southeast Kansas deserve more than coverage. Rudy believes they need uplifted, admonished, boosted, reminded, entertained and sometimes moved to tears or laughter.

He has been at his craft for more than 40 years, most of that time spent right at the desk of his hometown newspaper office.

His writing is a gentle read. It's the kind that makes your coffee get cold because you simply can't lay it aside until you're finished reading.

Rudy has my admiration because he chose small towns with names like Caney, Sedan, Edna, Chetopa, Cherryvale, Oswego and Altamont to carve out a living in country journalism. He could have climbed the ropes in bigger news organizations but he chose to spend his years working with his own family, keeping hometown newspapers in print, enlivening each one with writing that will never be famous because it is so local.

That's the way Rudy Taylor wants it.

You will see yourself in the pages of *Light On Main Street*. You will find your neighbors and kinfolks. You will rekindle thoughts of your own childhood.

Prairie beauty, through the eyes and the pen of Rudy Taylor, will leave you smitten with a longing to read another chapter about the joys and struggles of an editor in a small Kansas town.

Your coffee will get cold. That's a promise.

Introduction

At first, I thought light smelled like coal oil.

Our farm home in the Oklahoma hills didn't have electricity, so the amber light of coal oil lamps kept our family reading, playing, singing and generally contented during long evenings of the late 1940s.

I recall only flickers of the nightly routine, but they were indelibly etched in a little boy's mind. I remember the nightly ritual, especially during the wintertime when the sun set so early. My dad carried a coal oil lantern to do chores at the barn, always hanging it by the kitchen door as he came in for supper.

As he trudged toward the house, carrying that old green lantern, he would hear the voices of five children and a wife, all busily putting a meal on the table -- without the use of electricity.

He then saw light emanating from the kitchen windows. It wasn't bright. Just sufficient.

We didn't burn all our lamps at one time, so it made everyone cluster in the kitchen and dining room. That's where we read books, played the piano, studied and shared stories from our day at school.

Finally, as bedtime neared, my dad would carry a lamp to the bedrooms. He would carefully strike a kitchen match on the side of his pants, remove the globe of a bedside lamp, and set afire the little wick before carefully replacing the globe.

The bedroom lights did not burn for long. Everyone got ready for bed and one person in each room was given the job of blowing out the lamp. My older brother always tried to blow it out and jump in bed before the light went out. But he never made it.

As the youngest child in our family, I was the first to bed each night, giving me a unique perspective of the lamp dimming routine. The aroma of coal oil wafted gently through our house, and peaceful eyes soon closed, turning a page of one chapter in the life of a country family.

I saw the light, then it was gone. Then quickly came morning and the brilliance of another day.

Such has been my life, and I want to tell you about the wonderful lights I have experienced during my lifetime as a small-town editor.

So, sit back, dear reader. Slow your pace. Let your mind drift across the hills of Oklahoma and the rolling prairies of Kansas.

And, let me tell you about the *Light on Main Street.*

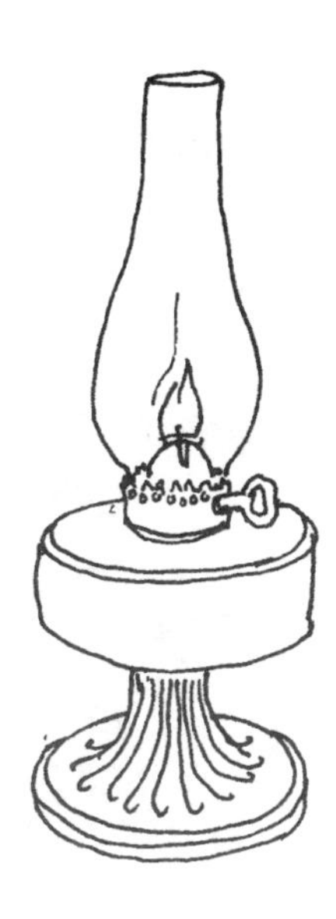

Mom's nightly thought: *Blow out your problems when you blow out the lamp.*

About this book

This is a book for enjoyable reading, nothing else.

It is non-fiction, but not a history book, therefore some of the names and places may not line up with reality.

One tip might be needed.

The chapters that are boxed with a gray screen were written "about" the hometown editor and you will notice the name of the town is never revealed. Those are the chapters that reveal the joys, struggles and challenges of publishing a country newspaper in the middle of America.

All other columns in *Light on Main Street* have been published in newspapers over the past 35 years, so the timelines may vary from the editor's younger days as a weekly newspaper editor to those he penned even this year.

Rudy Taylor in his Kansas newspaper office

CHAPTER ONE

Morning ritual

(Click)

A lamp on the editor's desk is the first light on Main Street. Merchants arrive one at a time, all of them looking up and down the street before they unlock their doors and start the daily chores of running their businesses.

Typically, they emerge within minutes with a broom in hand. The sidewalks and doorways get a good sweeping, and they pause momentarily to gaze at the empty storefronts where once teeming commerce took place.

They all carry a certain look of frustrating hope as they visit among themselves and grumble quietly about the big discount store in a nearby town that sucks the air out of their town.

Laughter can be heard as everyone goes about their day of selling groceries, hardware or clothing.

One of them glances toward the newspaper office and waves, knowing he is being observed, again, by an editor who admires them so much yet seldom joins the merchants' early morning ritual. He has been at his desk for an hour before there was one other light on Main Street, except for the headlights of the milk and bread trucks as they lined up at the local market.

Early morning writing, before staffers arrive and the telephone starts jingling, is something special to an editor. An editorial that has incubated in his mind is now on paper, and he carefully proofreads it, editing out words he would like to print but might cost him an advertising account up the street. After all, the mayor runs a clothing store and the barber serves on the school board.

He types "-30-" at the bottom of the piece and drops the editorial in the copy box where a middle aged woman typesetter has started working her way through stories that magically found their way into the little wire basket overnight. Some came through the mail and others were called to the editor at home.

A reporter brings in his journalistic cache after attending the city council meeting the night before. He also had stayed up late developing photos he took at the high school basketball game. It was quite a juggling act to take pictures during the first quarter, scribble a few notes, then head to the city meeting, then dart back to the school where a light still shone from the tiny window of the coach's office.

A small-town reporter knows the routine: Walk cautiously into that gymnasium and look at the faces of those leaving the school house. If the home crowd looks happy, it's OK to bounce into the coach's office and start firing questions. If they look forlorn, the reporter will keep a serious face and ask to see the score book. Nothing more. The picture and scores will tell the story to readers. Quotes from the coach will be delayed until another day.

It is now 8 a.m. at the newspaper office and the editor finally flips on the ceiling light in his office, alerting those who know him that his editorial is finished and his perusing of the checkbook has ended, at least until 3 o'clock when he knows a deposit must be made or else yesterday's payroll checks will bounce.

The little lamp on the desk seems to hunker. What was the light on main street an hour before now provides yellowish ambience to an office full of chatty voices, machines clacking and coffee cups clinking as everyone heads into another day in a country newspaper office.

Inspiring a writer

Being the last kid in the family had its advantages.

As a preschooler, I got to see something my brothers and sisters didn't get to witness -- watching our mother sit at the kitchen table and write.

After getting all the older children off to school, Mom would pour herself a cup of coffee, pull up a chair at the old, wooden table, and jot little lines of poetry.

They weren't much, and certainly never were intended to be published. Instead, they were destined for a lonely widow who lived up the road, a friend who was ill and had to miss Sunday church, or most often, a little line of hope intended to bring a smile to a nursing home resident.

Sometimes she would read them to me and I actually memorized some of them.

Day and night, just walk your mile,
With God's might, you'll keep your smile.

Admittedly, Mom didn't know a whit about feet and meter, and her poems would never win a literary prize. But as I look back at them, I realize they weren't penned to win contests. They were composed from the heart of a woman who cared about others.

She didn't realize it at the time, but Mom was not only uplifting lots of folks who really needed the boost, she also was inspiring a little boy to be a writer.

She often would take old greeting cards and cut the signature off the bottom, then scribble a note or poem on it.

Today, we would call that “re-gifting.” Actually, it was cheap. We didn’t have the money to buy cards.

Mom never considered herself to be a scribe of any caliber. She referred to it as “dabbling in poetry,” but I remember the joy her little lines brought to those who read them. We would get in the car and drive to a nearby nursing home, or stop by an elderly neighbor’s house and I would run up to the front door to deliver the written greeting.

We were a country version of a Hallmark commercial.

As I grew up in that home, I started jotting down my own thoughts and stashing them away. I still have many of them stored in a small, metal box. In some cases, I gave them to someone else. But mostly, I wrote them to bring light into my own life, not knowing that writing would become my passion. Maybe it was a genetic calling but I doubt it. Writing simply gives my life some purpose and an inner reward.

The Lane that Leads to Our House

The lane that leads to our house
is the prettiest place I know.
The trees on each side
of the road
stand proudly all in a row.

Entangled among them are vines and shrubs,
a dozen different kinds.
I love the lane in early spring,
it's hard to compare with anything.

The lane that leads to our house is the coolest lane I know,
when the sun beats down in August, it's the nicest place to go.
Two kinds of love birds call it home. One builds a nest
and sings a refrain.
The other drives slowly as if in a rain --- I think they call it
Lovers' Lane.

The lane that leads to our house is the prettiest place I know,
especially in winter when the trees are covered with snow.
The seasons may change the scene of the lane. They roll along
without one fear,
but the beauty it holds will never change, no matter the day,
no matter the year.

It's always that way,
on the lane that leads to our house.

(Grace Taylor - 1951)

"Off the Cuff"

Springtime in Witty's cellar

Each year when the nighttime thunderstorms move in, rumbling the windows and jarring awake even the heaviest sleeper, it unravels pleasant thoughts of yesteryear for me.

As a child, it wasn't uncommon for my brother, three sisters and myself to be awakened during the night by my mother with the stern announcement, "There's a storm moving in --- hurry, we're going to the cellar!"

To me, that was the best news my mom could bring, for I knew that in the cellar, located a half mile up the road behind the Witty's house, there would be at least two hours of childhood memories in the making.

My mother would gather up blankets so the kids could slumber in the cellar, and she would grab a few goodies from the kitchen counter just before pushing the kids out the door and dashing for the car through the rain.

My dad was always the first to the car, dependably nervous about the black, swirling clouds overhead. With seven of us crammed into our '36 Chevy we made the trip up the lane, across the highway and into the Witty family driveway. There, we would park alongside three or four other cars of neighbors who also utilized this hillside cellar which was a safe haven from even the worst of disasters.

Through the darkness, there was one sight we could depend upon -- Mr. Witty's lantern which he always waved from the cellar door. "Come on, come on in," he would predictably holler in his broken German accent. All seven of us would scurry inside where everyone would laugh at our wet clothes and hair and exchange neighborly talk with the already-seated inhabitants. It was like a party every time.

We called the twisting clouds cyclones instead of tornadoes, and even saying the word "cyclone" brought chilled talk and wide eyes from everyone in the semi-lighted cellar.

I can recall the children, including a couple cousins and other schoolmates of mine, wrapping up in the blankets on the damp floor. By the light of Mr. Witty's flickering lantern, the grown-ups would talk away the night, their voices bouncing off the rock walls like echoes in a canyon. I still call it "cellar talk" because those folks sounded so serious when they talked in the cellar during a storm.

They talked about spooky things, like the night my mother's family heard the piano playing down in the living room, but nobody was there playing it! Or, the night my uncle Arnold saw the panther up by the schoolhouse, or the wretched face which Mrs. Horton saw peering through her kitchen window once, and the tale about the big snake that squeezed ol' Ben Horton's leg until his foot turned as black as the snake. My sisters would cover their heads as Mrs. Washburn, a full blood Shawnee Indian, would reveal the visions she saw dancing in the clouds en route to the cellar that night.

Back then, it seemed like that cellar was cavernous, but it was probably no larger than most farm cellars. Still, the fact that it was built into the side of a hill made it such a warm and dry sanctuary from the pounding storm just outside.

It seemed that we stayed in there all night long, but it was no more than 30 minutes to an hour each time. I can recall how each of us held our breath as Mr. Witty opened the door at storm's end, fearing that the entire landscape would be flattened. Fortunately, it never happened that way.

Only last week, I drove back to my old home to see if the dogwoods were blooming, and the hillside by the Witty place was covered with the flowering trees. I noticed that the cellar had been bulldozed and replaced with some type of portable out-building.

Apparently, all the cellar dwellers are now gone.

Perhaps it was only a hole in a hillside, but to me it represented genuine legend-making. Those fables which were spun in that cellar, partly in jest and partly in earnest, were monumental events to the children who were fortunate enough to live in those simpler times, when a stormy night in the springtime turned into a harvest of childhood memories.

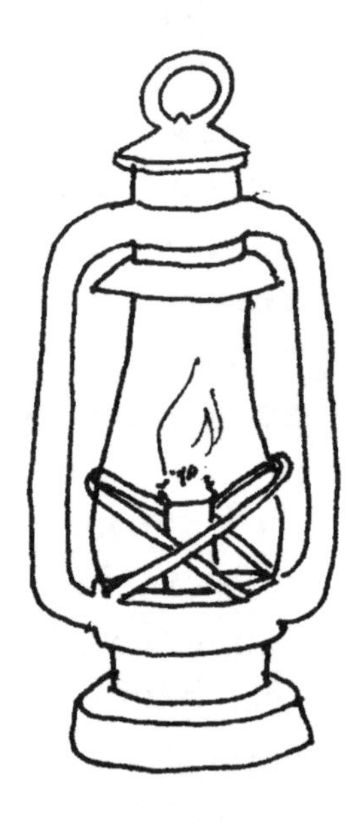

Celebrating freedom at the Big Rock

We called it "the big rock," and just saying those three words brings back such excitement to me.

The little community where we lived wasn't a town so we had no organized fire department to shoot off fireworks on the Fourth of July. We just rounded up a few aunts, uncles and cousins and headed to the *Big Rock* for a picnic. A nearby branch gave the kids a chance to go wading in what seemed to be clear water. The women brought lots of fried chicken, potato salad and other goodies.

If my dad had the money, he would buy a case of pop and a block of ice at the nearby country store.

When I look at how we decorate our homes today, complete with flags and bunting, each of our little towns having two or three huge fireworks stands, then skies above our communities are lighted with flashes, booms and screaming whistles, it makes those days at the *Big Rock* seem pretty plain.

Still, there was a sweet simplicity to those occasions, making them stand out in my mind as giants among my childhood memories. The extent of our fireworks were a few packages of ladyfingers and black cats. After dark, we would shoot a couple Roman candles and the kids would wave sparklers.

Period.

The thrill of the day came when my dad would reach into a big tub full of watermelons and pull out the biggest one -- cutting it into moon-shaped slices. We would salt the juicy, red melon then eat until we were stuffed.

Usually, all the cousins would join in a common whining session to "go swimming" at the nearby creek. And predictably, around mid-afternoon, our parents would give in and we would spend a few lazy hours relaxing in the shade of the big trees and wading in the fishy-smelling, muddy waters of Big Cabin Creek.

We didn't have television sets, so there were no golf matches, baseball games or patriotic programs to watch from distant cities. We didn't know the meaning of charcoaled anything. We munched on leftovers throughout the afternoon and evening.

So, there is reason for elation today. Fourth of July celebrations are more fun-packed, exciting and colorful than they were 50 years ago. And, quite frankly, I don't miss the mosquitoes from that muddy little creek one bit.

But when it comes to the *Big Rock*, I smile each time I think of it. It was simply a big flat sandstone, near a little brook, where tablecloths were spread, "grace" was said over the picnic food, and cousins ran through the woods and splashed in the shallow water.

There we celebrated the birth of a nation which made such precious freedoms possible.

The good of the day remains with us today.

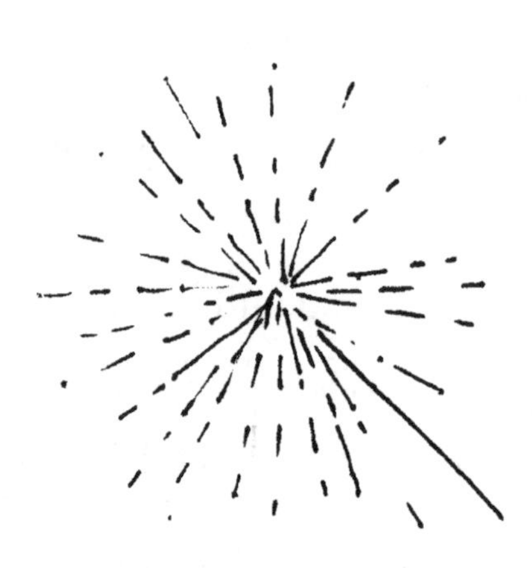

"Off the Cuff"

When did *Last Tag* die?

Somewhere in the past 50 years, *Last Tag* died.

Now, there was a game.

I never played halfback on a football team, never dunked a basketball or hit a home run. But I was pretty fair at *Last Tag*.

However, today I was crushed to find that my wife, who is my same age, claims no memory of *Last Tag*. She was a town kid and I was country boy.

I was born in a hilly community in Oklahoma, and I had a brother and three sisters. My parents, grandparents and great-parents on both sides also lived there. And, of course, that meant I had all kinds of aunts and uncles, and dozens of cousins.

Since we had no TV set, we spent many evenings visiting the homes of relatives and community friends. When the visits were over and the guests prepared to leave in their car, the children would play a simple game of tag. If you could tag another kid then jump in the back seat of your parents' car, you won. But usually it didn't go that way. One kid would tag another, then that kid would tag you "last tag" which invariably ushered in one last sprint to touch someone and holler, "Last tag on my tongue!"

Apparently there was something sacred about that little routine, because it was honored by all parties. Nobody dared touch you again if you tagged them then immediately grabbed your tongue while hollering, "Gotcha last tag on my tongue."

So, you can understand the consternation this morning when I kissed my wife goodbye and headed to the office.

"Tag," I said as I touched her arm.

"Huh?" she mumbled. "What's that mean?"

"You're supposed to tag me back," I said.

I ducked a couple of her attempts until she finally tagged me, at which time I uttered that mother of all phrases, "Gotcha last tag on my tongue." I grabbed the end of my tongue and held it as I ran from the house, jumped in my car and drove away.

I noticed a couple neighbors shaking their heads as they watched me start the car while holding tightly to my tongue.

See, the thing is, *Last Tag on Your Tongue* requires you to hold it while you count to one hundred.

Well, the day went just fine for this ol' editor, having won the little kitchen game this morning. It was later in the afternoon when our teenaged daughter came into my office and gave me a hug that things got a bit confusing.

"Mom says you really went bonkers this morning," she said. "You OK, Dad?"

"Me? Oh, sure, I'm fine. Mom just didn't grow up in Oklahoma where *Last Tag on Your Tongue* was an Olympic event."

There was silence, then she quietly left my office. I heard her tell her mother, in the other room, "Take away his sugar. Hide the Girl Scout cookies. And don't let him watch *The Waltons* tonight on TV.

She then whispered, "Dad's in another world."

I'll just skip the milk tonight

At the north edge of our town is a little barn where Red the cow and I held a secret for over 30 years.

As a 10-year-old boy, one of my nightly chores was to milk ol' Red. We became good friends, this cow and me. I can remember many winter evenings when the warmest place in the barn was at the right flank of my milk cow with her udder warming my cold hands, my head resting against the fur of her side.

My dad, who taught me to milk, gave me strict instructions on the importance or keeping the milk clean. In other words: Don't let the cow pee in the milk.

So, as I did my nightly milking, I always watched for the giveaway signs: Ol' Red would look up from her feed box and her eyes would start to water, then there was this straining sensation that could be felt from nose to tail, and sure enough ... the yellow river would start to flow.

My job, in such a predicament, was to jump back and remove the bucket from the general area, thereby keeping it sanitary and, hopefully, drinkable.

One evening, there must have been a pretty fourth grade girl on my mind because ol' Red looked up, her eyes watered, she strained mightily and I didn't notice.

I carried a bucket of yellowish milk to the house and my dad gave me a spanking. "I told you to watch for that," he said. He then took the bucket outside and poured the contaminated milk on the ground.

I learned a big lesson that night, because for the next several weeks I watched for pee signs, took diversionary moves and kept the milk supply worthy of our kitchen table or the butter churn.

Then one night it happened again. I was daydreaming about that darn girl again and it was a repeat performance for ol' Red. Well, my mama didn't raise any idiots and my plight wasn't a complicated one. I stirred the milk to hide the yellow, carried it to the house, and simply skipped the milk for a couple days.

I wasn't in the mood to get another spanking.

Ol' Red and me kept that secret for more than a quarter century until our family was enjoying a get-together one Sunday in the mid-1980s. My brother and sisters took turns telling tales of little episodes which we "thought" our parents didn't know about. Amazingly, the stories didn't surprise Mom and Dad one bit. They were pretty sharp parents.

Then I told my story about ol' Red and the funny-tasting milk.

It was a show stopper. Nobody thought it was funny. One of my sisters went running to the bathroom. I truly believe they all are still miffed about it, even today.

I never returned to drinking milk. Maybe it's because today's 1% and 2% milk is all watered down and tastes like nothing. But the truth is, one never knows when the milk boy of the previous day might have caught the fancy of a 10-year-old girl at school, and the watery eyes of his bovine might have gone unnoticed.

It's just easier to skip the milk.

CHAPTER TWO

The Chronicle has a life saver

She arrives an hour later than most staffers, mostly from habit after raising three children and taking them to school before heading to the office. But the hours she spends in the office are productive -- much more so than the editor's sashaying back and forth between his role as publisher and community servant.

Everybody looks to the local editor for information about the government. They want to know his opinion about the governor's plan to redo state highways. And they think he supports the president, regardless of which party is in power.

In truth, he simply wants to get enough ads pulled together to make possible another edition of the Chronicle. He knows there is sufficient news, sports, want ads and obituaries to fill the news hole. It's the ads that will generate the money to pay bills.

Still, when a state representative stops by, the newspaper editor must slow his feverish pace and gently listen, taking occasional notes to satisfy the politician's ego, and join in some grousing about "the gov'ment."

Meanwhile, his wife simply works.

She looks from her adjoining office and catches the editor's eye. She is tapping a red pencil with her finger which is a secret sign between this husband and wife team. It means, "I need help with the checkbook."

She then sticks her head in the door and quietly says, "You've got a phone call on the other line."

Funny. The Chronicle has only one telephone line.

Just before the newspaper is put to bed, someone hollers from the back, "Do we have *Lifesavers?"*

Everyone knows the answer. *Life's Little Lifesavers* is a column written by the editor's wife for most of her adult life. It consists of short but meaningful little phrases about life in a small town, and the Chronicle would be spiritless without it.

She holds out until the last minute to write it, not to show her power, but because her job as owner, bookkeeper and news writer is overwhelming. Besides, *Lifesavers* is a column that needs to be written under deadline, and she does, five minutes before the pages are sent to the print shop.

Everyone needs a lifesaver and the hometown Chronicle has one who writes a weekly column that lifts spirits and promotes gentleness and tranquility in daily living. A fourth generation Kansas journalist, Kathy Taylor is married to the author of "Light On Main Street."

"Off the Cuff"

The deadline and apple pie

It's the little things that make us glad that we returned to our hometown to publish this newspaper.

Yesterday was a nightmarish day in our office. Two staffers stayed home with the flu and our main typesetting machine went on the blink an hour before deadline.

That meant staying late, ordering pizza, and getting backaches from leaning over the paste-up boards until the newspaper was finished.

Discouraged and tired, we all looked at each other.

"Will we ever get there?" asked a young reporter.

Then the front door opened and we saw, and smelled, something unbelievable.

A husband-and-wife team who take a walk every night apparently saw the lights still glowing in our office. So, they went went back home and she made a homemade apple pie.

"We thought you might need to take a break," the woman said as she handed it to the editor's wife. "We don't know how you all do it -- printing our Chronicle every week. But we sure hope you never stop."

Suddenly, there was new life.

A fresh pot of coffee was brewed and everyone smiled and visited with these wonderful folks who brought hope into our lives at the very moment when we needed it most.

I took my pie into my office and watched through the open door as the staff bade the couple good night.

It's times like that when I feel like the king of the newspaper moguls, knowing fully that the night editor of the *Kansas City*

Star was probably chain smoking Camels and driving a herd of reporters as they prepared their morning edition.

I could imagine the *New York Times* publisher attending a star-studded opening of a Broadway show or sipping cocktails with the Secretary of State.

And, here I sat in my weekly newspaper office in a faraway little Kansas town, drinking hot coffee, listening to friendly laughter and eating apple pie.

The amazing thing is: This fine couple will never ask for anything in return. In their minds, they did nothing special at all.

That's why the Chronicle hit the streets today, just as it has for the past 120 years.

It will next week, too. And, the week after that. Until the day comes when nobody notices the little light on Main Street.

Life's Little Lifesavers

By Kathy Taylor

... the happy sounds of a baby laughing ... sunlight streaming through open curtains ... rising early ... remembering your first love ... comfy shoes ... the smell of an approaching rainstorm ... the ringing of church bells ... honesty ... the whistling of a tea kettle ... dozing in the recliner ... driving a clean car ... love notes ... crazy and silly times with your family ... a mother's hug ... playing basketball on the driveway ... finding the right screwdriver when you need it ... sipping coffee and daydreaming ... hearing a good friend's voice on the phone ... telling God about it, then listening as He talks.

"Off the Cuff"

A loaf of fresh bread is sure to make peace

Mom had a bread box on the kitchen counter when I was a kid, and I don't recall it ever being empty.

That's because my dad was like me today -- forgetful. As he drove home from work each evening, he would rack his brain trying to remember what my mom told him to bring home.

Dad would usually stop at the store and pick up a loaf of bread. It may have been corn meal or carrots that she asked him to get, but he always knew that toting a fresh loaf of bread would give him safe entry into the house.

Funny thing, I don't recall my mother complaining about his absent-mindedness. She just prepared more meals that required lots of bread.

I thought of that today when my wife told me her car needed gasoline. "We're going to Tulsa today," she said. "Would you mind filling the car with gas?"

Thirty minutes later I came back in the house all hot and sweaty. "Well, I got your car all washed and the windows are nice and shiny," I said with certain pride.

"You washed the car?" she asked. "I just spent five dollars last night washing the car and drying it off."

"Well, I just spent four more," I said with a grump. "So, now we have a nine dollar wash job."

We drove to Tulsa wearing frowns. Of course, we first stopped and filled the car with gasoline.

Last week, a local reader stopped by the Chronicle office to retrieve three photographs she had brought us the previous week. Problem was, I was holding down the fort by myself, and after looking through a stack of junk on my desk had to admit that the pictures were lost.

Or so I thought.

She just walked back to my desk, lifted one piece of paper, and there they were -- all three pictures.

I apologized to her as she left the office, looking back over her shoulder and dryly saying, "It's OK, Rudy. You can't help it."

And that reminds me of the story on television last week about the new security staffing at all U.S. airports. The perfect profile of a baggage screener was compiled and guess who it was? You guessed it -- a woman, age 45 to 60.

And, who has been screening most baggage in America's airports? Mostly men -- the ones who can't see a bottle of ketchup when it's perched right in front of them when they open the refrigerator door.

I notice stuff, too, but it's not important. I notice license plates and all the funny sequences of numbers and letters. I can tell you who polishes their shoes and who doesn't. Somebody once told me that people's underwear are just like their shoes, so I'm always curious to see who has scuffed and dirty loafers.

But I don't notice where I leave my keys or ball-point pen.

I stopped at a convenience store yesterday and bought a package of gum. When I paid for my purchase, the teenaged, female clerk quipped, "Here's your change, and don't forget your cell phone."

I looked at her sternly.

"What makes you think I'm the kind of guy who would lay down my cell phone and forget to take it with me?" I said.

"Because you're a man," she said. "You can't remember doo-doo."

That hurt, not just because she was one hundred percent right, but because she "didn't" say doo-doo. And I was on my way to church.

I noticed one thing: That little teenager had the same smirk on her face as the reader who snatched her photos from my office desk. It's a look women seem to wear when they talk to me. They act like I'm an ol' coot.

Well, I'll show them.

As soon as I find my glasses and ball-point pen, I'll make a list, and tomorrow I shall follow it to a "T."

But just to make sure I'm covering all the bases, I'll probably walk in the front door tonight carrying a loaf of bread.

It's not much of a game plan, but it works.

Or at least, she let's me think so.

CHAPTER THREE

He came home

"Editor" seems to suit him, but he certainly never started out to be one.

People often ask if he likes living in the town where he grew up and publishing the weekly Chronicle.

"I love it," he will say with a smile and nod. But inside he reels with another thought. "Good grief. I'm trapped here in this dusty little town."

He flirted with radio while in college and liked his job as announcer and newsman for a couple different stations. After college he worked for a large oil company, writing broadcast commercials, print ads and speeches for executives who were on their way to speak at Rotary meetings or state conventions of oil patchers.

It wasn't in his plan to return to the small town where he grew up and run a newspaper that always seemed corny to him. Once, when he was in college, he recalls the journalism professor asking all the students to bring a copy of their hometown newspaper to class. He was embarrassed to stand before Reporting 113 class and hold up a six-page edition of the Chronicle. He mumbled something about "the gossip sheet" before handing it to his professor.

While other students showed off their hometown papers, many of them ten times bigger than the Chronicle, he noticed the professor wasn't paying attention. He was buried on page 2 of the tiny Chronicle, his eyes sweeping back and forth as he read *The Happy Corner,* a column written by Skeet George, its owner and editor. Mr. George also happened to be the embarrassed student's father-in-law and his mentor in life. But he didn't think anyone would be interested in knowing about that.

Class ended and the professor hollered at him. "Hey, do you know this guy?" He held up the Chronicle and pointed to the editorial page.

"Sure, that's ol' Skeet George. Pretty simple stuff, isn't it?"

The professor handed the Chronicle back to him and replied, "That's the beauty of him -- his writing is simple yet magnetic. I couldn't put it down until I finished *The Happy Corner.*"

It was a life changing moment for the student. He took the newspaper back to his apartment, sat down and read the column and two adjacent editorials over and over.

Skeet George loved his town. His family and neighbors adored him. He loved the country newspaper business. And, it was obvious he loved to write.

The journalism professor nailed it. There was magnetism in the writing found in that little newspaper, and it began to work on the young journalist's mind as he finished his education and started looking for a future in advertising, public relations or technical writing. He was totally unaware of the pull toward his hometown that finally resulted in Skeet George saying those magic words: "Are you at all interested in taking over the Chronicle?"

He didn't have to ask twice.

Today, the young journalist who is approaching retirement age himself, often closes his eyes and thinks about the world he missed, the money he might have made, and the retirement condo he might have owned in the Colorado Rockies by now.

His oft-heard comment: “I like where I live and what I do at least five days a week. The other two days -- I wish I had stayed with the big oil company.”

He figures that isn’t a bad percentage.

“If it ever turns around the other way, I’ll leave in a second.”

But today he is surrounded by a son and daughter who have come back to join the family publishing business, and his wife of 40 years still believes in him. Another son lives in a nearby town where he works in banking.

They are his fortune, his retirement fund, his mountain home with a view.

And now that grandchildren come running through the front door of the newspaper every day, he has totally thrown in the towel.

The lights that illuminate his world cast no shadows. They are the people, family, neighbors and readers of the hometown Chronicle. And he savors every minute spent in what he once considered a dusty little town.

"Off the Cuff"

One long and two shorts meant it was OK to answer

If there's one thing that's all-American, it is the telephone. Irritating as this gadget can be, I can't fathom spending one day without one.

As a boy, our first telephone hung on the wall and looked like something straight out of *Mayberry RFD*.

It was big and mostly made of oak. On the side was a crank with a handle and it was our only way of signaling the outside world that we wanted to talk.

The whole thing worked this way: You walked up to the telephone and retrieved the ear piece, which was a black thing that was used only for listening. You took it off its hook and placed it to your ear, carefully listening to make sure the line wasn't already in use. If it was, you had two options: Either hang up and wait your turn, or quietly listen to a couple of neighbors as they chatted on the party line.

My mom liked to do that, and she always claimed one neighbor lady was making time with a farmer up the road while both their spouses were at work.

Of course, at age eight, that didn't interest me, but I can remember the whispered stories Mom would tell her friends the next day.

The speaking piece was separate -- a round, tin-can looking device that was permanently mounted on the front of the wooden box. With one hand holding the ear piece and standing tiptoed to place your mouth close to the speaking piece, you could have a conversation with distant friends.

Rural telephone lines were privately owned and weren't anything close to today's twisted wire cables that carry thousands of conversations over one little wire. Old copper lines were about the gauge of the bail on a paint bucket and they zigzagged across the countryside, sometimes on legitimate poles but often meandering to an insulator nailed to a barn or a tree that had been stripped of its limbs.

While our friends in town enjoyed good telephone service, most rural conversations took place over the sound of an incessant roar on the line. So conversations were kept short. There was no such thing as a quiet talk with a friend. Hollering over the speaking piece was the common strategy.

After listening to make sure the line wasn't being used, you hung up the ear piece and turned the crank several rotations to make sure "central" got the signal. Central was the operator in town and she would come on the line with an all-business tone to her voice as she said, "Number, please?"

At that point, you announced the number you wanted to reach. "Two two four," you'd say if you wanted to call that number, and a jingle was heard on the other end. Then the conversation began. However, if you wanted to reach someone on your own line -- and it wasn't uncommon to have six or eight neighbors on that line -- you simply turned the crank in coded fashion to make them answer.

For instance, our ring was one long and two shorts. You didn't have to go through Central if you knew the rings -- and we all knew them by memory.

Your phone rang often, but most of the time it was for another neighbor, not you or anybody in your family. And sometimes, after hearing a neighbor's ring several times, a friendly neighbor would pick up the phone and announce, "The Taylors are at church and won't be back until around eight."

Back then, we had Voice Mail, Call Waiting and Caller ID -- we just didn't know it. In truth, the operator kept pretty good track of her customers.

Before we'd go on vacation, my mother would call Central and tell her our plans. The operator used discretion in telling others about our whereabouts, but felt the freedom to tell a caller if it might keep a caller from worrying.

Central also would call us at a friend's house if she knew that's where we happened to be.

The hometown operator also served as disciplinarian for kids who might spend too much time on the phone. She also would tell the parents when kids used the phone as a toy. More than once, an old fashioned telephone operator saved the life of a person who was experiencing a medical emergency.

In the small town where I lived, the operator also maintained the official "switch." It looked like a regular light switch, but the plate was painted red and the words above it simply read, "Whistle." It was the fire siren which brought out all the volunteer firemen anytime they heard it roar. But it also signaled noontime in our town. The operator watched her clock and gave the noon whistle one good blast so local folks and nearby farmers would know it was time for lunch.

Today, I carry a cell phone, Palm Pilot, laptop computer, iPod, satellite radio and a notebook with a built-in calculator. I keep hearing that a new gadget even incorporates a tiny TV screen in the cell phone, along with a movie camera and built-in credit card.

That's OK, I suppose. But life was pretty good for those of us who grew up in small towns and rural areas where wooden telephone boxes with funny looking ear pieces and wind-up handles gave us our first glimpse of the world up the road a ways.

Neighbors knew neighbors because we listened to their conversations, and nobody would dare say a curse word on the phone because Central would cut us off, call our parents and give us a good scolding the next time we tried to make a call.

Makes us sound downright uncivilized today, doesn't it?

He-Cola and She-Cola

Watching youngsters get their county fair animals ready to show always conjures good memories. But I never see a twin calf category in summer fairs, and there really should be one.

I was only six when my dad came to the breakfast table one summer morning and announced, "The old brindle cow had twins last night. I had to carry them both to the barn, but I don't think the baby calves will make it. The mama cow is rejecting them."

Then he said those magic words: "Somebody will have to bottle-feed them and I just don't have the time."

I immediately jumped up from the table and headed out the door, hollering over my shoulder, "Don't let them die! I'll feed them!"

Looking back, I'm sure my dad and mom cooked up that little scheme. They weren't the type to let two tiny calves die. They just knew I needed some motivation. And it worked.

I named them He-Cola and She-Cola.

For the next few weeks, my dad would get me up early so I could bottle feed the twins, then that evening I would repeat the feeding.

I didn't think those bucket calves would ever get big enough to start eating regular feed, but they did. One was a bull calf and the other a little heifer. We kept She-Cola and two years later she became a mama herself. He-Cola went to the sale barn, netting me seventy-five cents ... and a load of tears as I gave him up.

It was a good lesson in life for me. I learned that life has value and nobody should ever give up on those who are weak. I learned the importance of getting up early and doing chores, right alongside my dad. And I learned that personal dedication to someone else -- even if it's a couple lonely calves -- is always worth the effort.

He-Cola and She-Cola simply wanted to live. They had no idea why their mother had rejected them or who might bring them a bucket with a built-in nipple to provide each day's sustenance. But it wasn't long before the sound of my voice and the banging of that bucket brought them running to the barn and two little twins grew bigger.

The mere fact that I remember their names some 55 years later tells me it was a life-changing summer for a little boy and a pair of brindle-colored calves.

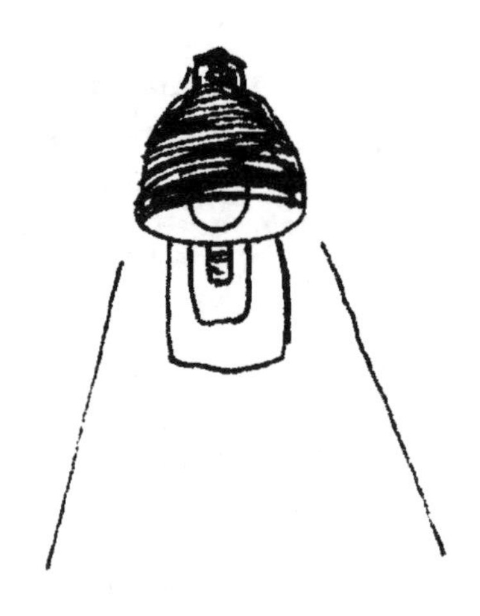

"Off the Cuff"

Learning about romance at the country pie supper

A reader came in the office this week to run a notice about a pie supper.

"Do you suppose anybody remembers what that is?" she asked with a chuckle. And my mind went spinning back, as it often does these days.

The country school I attended in the early 1950s was known for its annual pie supper, held in November, just before Thanksgiving. It was our community's social event of the year, and I well remember the three-room schoolhouse being packed to capacity with kids, parents and neighbors as they swapped stories, laughed together, and admired the pies and box suppers that graced two long tables in the front of the room.

Just driving up to the school was an experience in itself -- it created a surrealistic scene for the kids who seldom saw the building with lights glowing in yellowish hue through the windows.

Cars parked all over the school grounds.

Of course, the men in the crowd knew the pie supper rules: They were expected to bid on "certain" pies, baked to perfection by their wives, girlfriends, mothers and daughters. And, predictably, some ornery friend would run up the bid, dropping out just in the nick of time.

It was quite a routine, one which continued in that community until the school finally closed in the early 1960s.

But it wasn't the men and their pies that created my lifetime memory. It was one particular box supper that I knew had my name on it. My only classmate in the first grade (there were four grades in the room) was a girl named Linda, and she had gone to great lengths to make sure I knew her box would be wrapped in orange paper with a white bow on top.

I thought the auctioneer would never finish selling pies, the proceeds of which went to buy Christmas candy to be given out during the upcoming Christmas season. He looked over the table and boomed out, "OK, folks, here's a pretty little box supper that some little girl has prepared just for somebody special. The top bidder will get to share the contents of this box with ... little Linda over here!" He pointed to the pretty first grader who was by then blushing.

My dad poked me in the ribs. "I think you've got a bid of a dime over here," he hollered, and he raised my hand up. "One dime has been bid," the auctioneer continued, "do I hear twenty cents?"

To my shock, a voice from the back pierced the crowd noise, "I'll bid thirty-five cents!"

"Don't look back there," my dad whispered. "There will be other boxes."

I reached in my pocket and looked at the three dimes my dad had given me. I was already out of the bidding, and my heart was aching.

But just as the auctioneer was about to holler "sold!' to the unknown bidder from the back, I felt two more dimes drop into my hand.

"Fifty cents!" I hollered with the shrill excitement of a confident first grader.

"I've got a half dollar right over here," the auctioneer shouted. "Do I hear a higher bid?" and he immediately tapped the gavel, never giving the other guy a chance to respond.

My dad gave him a smile and nod of approval.

Well, little Linda and I probably didn't say two words as we shared a desk and ate our ham sandwich and pumpkin pie. But it was a night to remember.

I have no idea if "Linda" still lives in these parts, or for that matter, remembers that pie supper held in the fall of 1953 in that little country school. All I know is this: A pretty little girl, a crafty auctioneer and a thoughtful and romantic dad made it into a memorable evening for a boy who ran short on dimes, but had the good fortune of being the recipient of immeasurable love --- and a pretty good piece of pumpkin pie, too.

The Timber Hill School today is in shambles, but a nostalgic editor still enjoys walking across the grounds and recalling the memories of his childhood.

"Off the Cuff"

Little hobgoblins can leave a lasting impression on old folks

I held hands with my sisters Shirley and Karen during my first trick-or-treat experience.

I was five at the time. They were older. And I thought holding hands with them was cool.

Good grief.

We walked from our farm home about a quarter mile to an older couple's house. I wore a hand-me-down mask and my mother tied strings of tin cans and crepe paper cutouts around my neck. I don't remember what the girls wore. Fact is, at that point in my life, I hadn't even noticed they were girls. They were appendages, attached to me every step I took. And that certainly was the case that Halloween evening at dusk as we walked up that dark lane toward the old German couple's house.

Looking back, I think they took me along for strength, because the house was more than a little bit scary. The old folks didn't have electricity, so the coal oil lamp in the window cast an eerie glow onto the big front porch.

We lined up in front of their door and quietly practiced our lines.

Shirley would say "trick."

I would say "or."

And Karen would follow with "treat."

Rehearsal complete, we knocked on the big door, then waited as footsteps were heard inside and the porcelain door knob turned. The door hinges squeaked and the little lady appeared in the dim light of the doorway.

We nervously did our trick-or-treat line, and Mrs. Witty invited us in.

Of course, she knew we would be coming. No doubt, we were the only kids to knock on their door that night.

The old gentleman was sitting in his big rocking chair by the potbellied stove. He leaned over the right side of the chair and spat tobacco juice into the spittoon.

"Come over here, kids," he said in his broken German accent. "Come into the light where I can see you."

Our hands were sweaty as we took three steps forward and faced the old couple who handed each of us a sack of homemade cookies. Mine had a wooden whistle inside, too -- one Mr. Witty had apparently whittled from his predictable perch on the front porch of that old house.

We didn't stay long, and we so enjoyed eating those cookies on our walk back down the hill to our house.

But my greatest memory of that night was not the treat in my sack, or the crazy mask I wore, or the spooky walk up those front steps. What I remember most were the glistening eyes and smiles of an old couple who had looked forward all day long to that knock on the door, knowing there would be youth in their living room, if only for a few minutes.

As I grow older, I find my own face lighting up when I'm in the presence of children. And, tonight we will spend an entire evening answering our front door, handing out treats, and trying to guess the identity of each little hobgoblin who rings our doorbell.

My greatest hope is that they will see how happy they made us, just as I remember that night more than a half century ago when three country kids spoke three words and illuminated the lives of two special old friends.

There's nothing spooky about such special times.

CHAPTER FOUR

An editor with a shadow

He stands at his desk and stares at the irregular hangings of plaques on his office wall -- from the Jaycees, 4-H club, fair board, press association, parent/teacher organization.

But the one he holds more valuable than any other is actually a piece of paper that he keeps folded and hidden in his top desk drawer. It is a finger painting by his youngest son --- the one who now is 35 and serves as Chronicle editor.

It shows a dad with a pipe in his teeth. Below it are haunting words for the old man. *Dad – I want to be just like you.*

This starts a predictable ritual for the publisher, one where he glances at the decoupaged plaque from his wife, just telling him he's a winner in her book. Beside it is one with a saying by Abraham Lincoln: *I like to see a man proud of the place he lives, and so live that the place is proud of him.*

His eyes move to the plaque that speaks his heart -- a simple poem written nearly a century before by an author named Henry Van Dyke:

Time is:
Too Slow for those who Wait
Too Swift for those who Fear
Too Long for those who Grieve
Too Short for those who Rejoice
But for those who Love
Time is not.

And, finally, he glances at the little saying: *Most people are just about as happy as they make up their minds to be.*

He smiles at that one, then returns to his typewriter.

There's a town out there that awaits the weekly Chronicle like they hunger for ice cream, only a bit more slyly. Who really wants to say they can't wait for the local paper to come out? It's mostly gossip, they will say. It only confirms what you've already heard. Its editorials are slanted to the right. The left. The middle road.

The clock now reads 6:30 and the telephone jingles. "Are you coming home for supper?" his wife asks in a monotone voice with a hopeful rise at the end.

She knows the answer. "Go ahead without me. I'll warm it up when I get home."

Then he says those cursed words: "Time got away from me today."

He steps into the adjoining office where the light still burns. The young editor is packing his camera into a bag and getting ready to head out to a meeting. "You still here?" he says without looking up.

"Yea, I've still got to go through the checkbook again. I'm way off on the balance."

"You've been reading those wall plaques again, haven't you?" he says with a grin.

Out the door he goes, leaving his own home fires to burn on their own, repeating the same dreadful mistakes his dad made when he was young.

"Where have the years gone?" the older editor quietly mumbles.

He takes one more look at his wall, then clicks off the light, locks the front door and starts the five-block walk home.

She will be glad to see him walk through the door.

He knows that.

But he wonders as he walks, "Why on earth would any little boy want to be just like me?"

"Off the Cuff"

The aroma of gasoline and soda pop made a pit stop into an adventure

Start a conversation at the coffee shop about the price of gasoline and the subject of gas wars always comes up.

You know the routine.

One guy says, "I remember when gasoline was only thirty cents a gallon." To which his buddy replies, "Heck, I remember when it was a quarter."

With bidding open, someone invariably remembers when gasoline sold for 19 cents, then the bragging comes to an end when a know-it-all announces, "I remember a gas war in Wichita (it was always someplace out of town) when they gave away the gasoline and just charged tax."

Regardless, I'm wondering what ever happened to gas wars.

Today, the signs look like clones of each another as you drive along a highway. If one place offers gasoline at $2.09, you can depend on every neighbor's sign reading the same.

Maybe communication is better these days, suppose?

Of course, the price of gasoline has, from its first days nearly a century ago, been priced with a ".9" at the end. I've always thought our ages should be expressed like gasoline: "How old am I? Why, I'm thirty-nine ... nine!"

Sure, sure.

When I was growing up, and during my first 20 years of driving, there was no such thing as self-service. In fact, a little sticker on gasoline pumps said, "State law prohibits customers from dispensing gasoline without assistance."

Try driving up to your local convenience store today, honking and waiting at the pump. You'll die of starvation.

There was only full service in those days.

You'd drive up to the pump, wait until the friendly gas jockey came out, then you'd roll down your window and announce, "I'll have two dollars worth of regular, please."

That would buy you at least eight gallons of gas.

Then you'd watch as the attendant washed all your car windows, checked the oil and battery, gave the fan belt a couple tugs, checked the air in all four tires, wiped his hands then calmly said, "Would you like your floorboards swept out?"

As a kid, I always associated getting a fill-up with soda pop, because sometimes my dad would spring for a bottle of the liquid refreshment as we listened to the gas pump quietly go "clang, clang, clang."

Filling station soda pop was the best you could buy.

I don't recall anybody ever getting rich running a filling station, so I know that their margin of profit wasn't very high. Even today, government regulations have made selling gasoline into a six-figure investment, so nobody is making their fortune selling this juice that is so popular with all of us.

So be nice to your friendly convenience store owner. It ain't easy to make a living, regardless of what you're peddling.

But I can say this without hesitation: Getting a fill-up was once an adventure. Today, it's a chore.

I suppose there's an option to it all. Nobody is holding a gun to our heads and making us buy those gas-eating pickups, SUVs and motor homes. We pull up to the gasoline pumps, stick a credit card in the slot, and watch the numbers on the pump fly by so fast it makes us dizzy. We ignore our tires and oil, sometimes smear some dirty water on the windshield, seldom wave at the convenience store employee, then head on down the road. It's a ritual we repeat without much thought.

We usually skip the soda pop in these modern times. It's just a good way for a 60-year-old guy to spill sticky stuff on his shirt as he drives. In the old days, you drank the pop from a bottle, and you did it at the station. After all, it cost an extra two cents to take the bottle with you.

Of course, by now, this story is starting to get boring to the younger folks.

It's that way when you're under age twenty-nine ... nine.

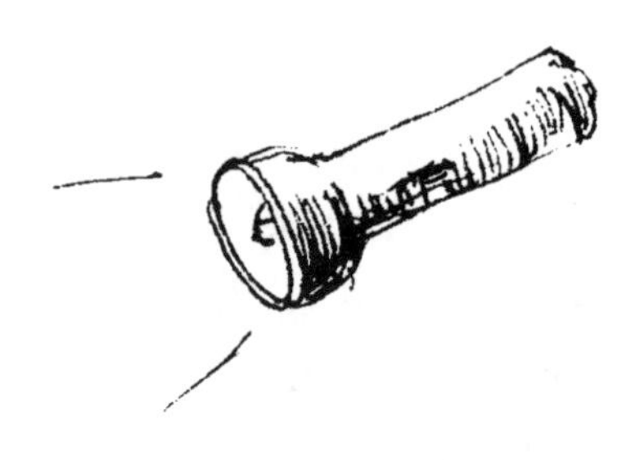

"Off the Cuff"

Gerber jars, Pat Boone and pop bottles to buy the groceries

A wealthy stock broker gave Dustin Hoffman one word of advice in the 1968 movie, *The Graduate*.

Plastics.

The old guy told the young college graduate that he was entering an adult world where plastic would rule. Virtually everything would be made of the stuff.

Boy, was he right.

Last week, the Gerber Company announced that it would no longer pack its baby food in glass jars. The familiar jars will be replaced with squared-off, plastic containers.

I find that bit of news to be rather distressing. What man doesn't have a shelf in his garage with Gerber lids nailed to the bottom-side, then the jars are suspended underneath and loaded with screws, nails, tacks and washers. And every good seamstress stores her buttons, snaps and sequins in a Gerber jar.

Now, the Gerber jars will look like medicine bottles -- square ones.

I've never gotten along well with plastic. I break little tabs, squeeze and spill beverages served in flimsy plastic cups, and I spend half my time picking up itt-bitty pieces of plastic Styrofoam from my lawn -- fragments from coffee cups, if that's what you want to call them.

I call them an icky way to serve coffee. A good cup of java should always be served in a glass, china or ceramic cup.

But I also hold similar hang-ups about mustard, barbecue sauce, salad dressing and shoe polish. And whoever dreamed up soda pop in plastic bottles must have been on drugs. A 6 oz. Coca-Cola, back when I was growing up, was the most delicious thing in the world. Now they sell Coke in 2- and 3-liter plastic bottles, and it all tastes flat. Plus, there's way too much of it in a bottle.

Besides, what does a kid do in this day and age when he needs a few nickels or dimes to buy something? As a boy, I sold pop bottles back to the grocer for two cents apiece. Even when my wife and I were newlyweds, there were lots of times when we didn't have a penny to our name, but we usually had a back porch full of pop bottles. More than once, we bought our groceries from the sale of pop bottles.

Try selling a plastic bottle. Yeah, sure.

I'm also hacked that all the car companies have removed the genuine chromium molding that once made automobiles so beautiful. They're now plasticized, inside and out. And, anybody who has ever tried to replace screws under the dash of their car knows how many extra plastic clips remain on the floor when the job is done.

I'm a nut. Everybody knows that. If I drink milk, I insist that it be served in a tall, cold clear glass -- even crystal when it's available. I make the checkout clerk use paper sacks for our groceries. I never allow a hamburger to be placed in a styrofoam box. And every time I unpack a computer, radio or clock and find it packed with those silly plastic peanuts, I go bonkers.

I think drinking glasses should glisten. Ice cubes should clink when they are served. Ketchup shouldn't be squeezed like toilet paper. And Gerber baby food should be lovingly spooned directly out of little, round jars.

God made them that way.

"Off the Cuff"

You can't shoot 'em down over Yukon

Everyone in our home, but probably nobody else in the world, says this little phrase: *You can't shoot 'em down over Yukon*.

It's our way of saying, "Hey, let's move on -- you can't cry over spilled milk."

You know the thought. Everybody has their way of expressing it.

"Keep your head up."

"Climb right back into that saddle."

"Shrug it off."

"Step over it."

"Forget about it!"

It was almost 40 years ago that I worked as a booth announcer for KWTV television in Oklahoma City. As I gave live commercials and station promotions from my microphone, I occasionally would stumble over a word.

That's when I would hear the calm words of my director through my headphone. With his southern drawl, Billy Bob Brown would simply say, "Keep going, Rudy -- you can't shoot 'em down over Yukon." Of course, nobody heard him except me, but it always gave me the confidence to keep going.

Here's the way director Brown explained it: "There are lots of times when you'd like to run outside the TV station, take a shotgun and shoot those words down before they head out to the towns of Oklahoma," he said. "But by the time you say them, they're already over Yukon or Bristow or Enid.

"... and you can't shoot 'em down over Yukon."

I don't know about you, but I have a stewing problem. When I mess up or bumble my way into trouble, I have a tendency to chew my cheek and crinkle my brow.

That's when my wife will walk by me, pat my bald head and say, "Whatever that is on your face, remember -- you can't shoot 'em down over Yukon."

As a small-town editor and publisher, there have been times that I took one glance at our front page and wished I could run out and buy every copy of my own newspaper, just to avoid the embarrassment of a mistake.

Unfortunately, once it's in print, it is there forever. I empathize with old-time editors whom I never knew. Anytime I look through century-old editions of our newspaper, I see mistakes, wrong information and hastily composed opinions. Those editors probably did the same thing that all members of our publishing family do every week -- we throw the paper across the room and turn red-faced.

It may be a blurred photograph, a wrong headline over the right story, a misspelled name of a well-known resident, a blob of black ink on the homecoming queen's face, or an editorial that didn't get the required incubation time before getting printed.

Mistakes in a newspaper are indelible. Sure, we can run a retraction, but the old story, the one with the "xmxmxmxm" that we had planned to replace with a real name when we found the proper spelling, remains in magazine racks, boxes, and in our case, microfilm for the historical society to keep for another century.

I think that's why I love the story in the Bible where it says our Heavenly Father forgives and forgets our sins. They're placed "from east to west," the Good Book says.

I don't know how heavenly our family saying might be, but it still helps to repeat our pet phrase when wrong words find their way into print -- probably even today's edition.

Billy Bob Brown was right: You'd like to do it, but you just can't shoot 'em down over Yukon.

Of course, if I did manage to do it, my words would probably fall right across the Yukon water tower and ooze down the sides in big red letters for everyone to see.

Newspaper folks can't run fast enough to shake the words that follow after us.

A slip of the tongue made him want to take a shotgun and blast the words out of the sky over the plains of Oklahoma. But "you can't shoot 'em down over Yukon," he learned from a wise director.

CHAPTER FIVE

The local cafe

Small towns can smother an editor. Really suffocate him.

It's not that people in these towns are small thinkers because they're not. They just have a way of diminishing the job of newspaper editor to one who gives their clubs and churches free publicity and gets the facts mixed up when they bring in news articles. Or so they think.

When a newspaper family goes to a local restaurant, there emerges a constant line of people who stop by their table to say hello. And that's the beauty of living in a small town. Most people are friends.

Still, there is a notion out there that editors know everything, and if not, they want to know everything. They also assume the fellow who publishes the local Chronicle has an opinion on every issue in the world.

"So, what do you think of this governor we just elected," a friend will ask as he pulls up a chair at the restaurant. "Isn't it just like a politician to ride the fence until he gets elected?"

"Mmmm, yeah, he's quite the guy," the editor responds while stirring his soup. "Your family doing OK?"

"You mean nobody has told you?" the table visitor says.

"I guess not," the editor responds.

"Boy, oh boy, I thought newspaper editors knew everything!" He then goes into a hilarious laugh, causing folks at the adjoining table to join in.

"My grandson got a full ride scholarship to Bethel College up in Newton."

"Oh, that's wonderful, the editor's wife chimes in. "We're all so proud of him."

"You hardly ever mention his name in the paper," says the proud grandpa. "But I suppose that's because I don't run a downtown business or place big ads in your paper."

There is silence.

"Good to see you," the editor says with finality.

He looks at his soup, knowing it is cold by now.

"We should have driven over to Coffeyville for dinner," he tells his wife. "At least they leave us alone in Coffeyville."

Then comes a local minister.

He exchanges pleasantries and hands the editor a photocopied story from his denomination's state newsletter.

"I thought you might want to put this in the Chronicle," he said. "You know, the homosexuals are taking over everything, and it doesn't help that the United Nations just bought the Grand Canyon."

"We'll look it over," says the editor's wife who grabs the paper.

"We were just about ready to say grace."

"Oh, sure, sure," the parson quietly says before leaving.

"If one more person comes to our table and keeps us from eating, I'm going to scream," the wife says.

"Well, well," comes a booming voice. "Hey, everybody. You'd better watch what you say tonight. The editor is here!"

There is nervous laughter in the little cafe.

The Chronicle owners leave, still hungry.

"Don't let them bother you," he tells his wife who is steaming. "They really do like us."

As they get in their car to leave, they see another car pull up and the driver rolls down his window. "Take out the ad on the trailer house," he hollers. "But leave in the want ad for a good bird dog."

He zooms out of the parking lot.

"Who was that?" the editor asks his wife.

"Heck if I know."

"How am I going to know which ad to pull and which bird dog ad he's talking about," the editor asks.

"That's why we come here every other night to eat," she says. "So people can line up and straighten us out."

They head back to the Chronicle office for some after-supper writing.

On the way to town, they stop at a drive-in and pick up a couple burgers and fries.

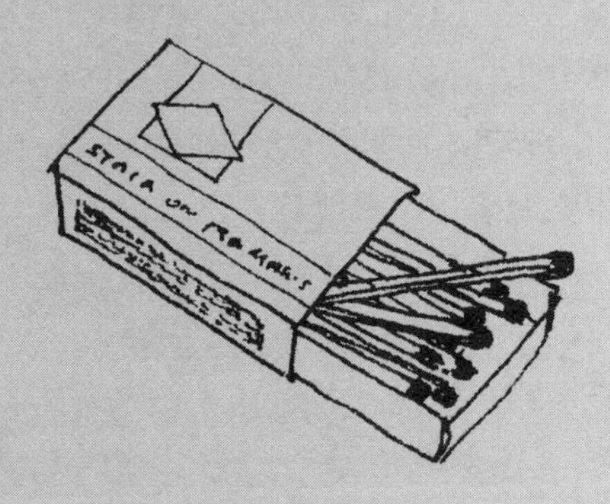

"Off the Cuff"

Flowers in my trombone

I changed the flowers in my trombone today --- my contribution to springtime.

No doubt, I'm the only newspaperman in America who keeps a 1932 Buescher trombone hanging upside-down on my office wall. It's my way of celebrating those wonderful years I spent in grade school, high school and college playing that old axe, and I mark the changing of seasons by sticking an arrangement of silk-but-seasonal flowers in the bell of the old horn. It makes me smile when I look at it.

But it also makes other people shake their heads and crinkle their brows as they stare at my crazy wall creation.

An area woman came to the office this week to give me a piece of her mind because I dared to say something good in print about President Clinton.

She ended her hands-on-hips monologue with this quip: "You're a liberal Democrat nut ... and I also think the daisies in your trumpet look stupid!"

Believe me, it's not the first time a fellow Republican has given me heck for fellowshipping the Demos, and I can overlook the fact that she didn't know that my new spring flowers were silk zinnias. But she called my Model 400 Buescher trombone a trumpet!

For that, she will answer on the judgment day. I'm sure of it.

* * *

That old horn was 25 years old when my parents bought it for me for $60. The previous owner was the first trombonist for the Tulsa Philharmonic Orchestra, and he played during the war years in various big bands in the Tulsa area.

I often look at the old horn and wish it could talk or play out what it has seen. Did its first owner stand on the refrain of Glenn Miller's *In The Mood,* and did it sound best with a mute in its bell?

I recall my first lessons, and sounding like a sick calf as I tried to punch out a B flat. But I also remember those years in the local high school where a wonderful conductor pulled fantastic sounds from a bunch of average student musicians.

I remember playing in the Serenaders dance band in that school and hearing the applause as I lugged through a solo at the beginning of *The Nearness of You*.

My arms still ache from memories of hauling that horn in its heavy case to marching events in tiny towns, as well as big university band days.

I recall some pretty salty sounds emitted from that Buescher as I played in a Dixieland band during college.

I feel lucky that I have my old trombone to keep me company when feisty old Republicans pounce on me; or when a cranky reader calls to remind me how many typos she counted in last week's Chronicle; or when the banker calls to remind me of an overdue note.

During such moments, I can lean back in my lumpy desk chair, stare at my 1932 upside-down trombone with red and purple zinnias sticking out the bell, and smile at the storm.

And I only get mad when some oaf calls it a trumpet.

"Off the Cuff"

Night-walking in our town

My world slows each evening as I take a one-mile walk around the streets of my hometown. It is partly exercise and partly stress relief. But it also has another effect that my neighbors probably don't know about ... I do some innocent gazing. Snooping would be more accurate.

One learns a lot by taking a night-time walk on residential streets.

I look at lawns and wonder why more people don't trim around trees. I see the junk that's stashed beside houses and I peer inside garages while clipping along in my tennis shoes, baggy shorts and sweaty t-shirt.

I hear voices from inside houses, and can tell you who fights and who talks nicely to other family members.

The smell of supper time permeates the air and I could make a list of who eats salmon cakes and who throws a few sliced onions in with their fried potatoes.

Dogs run the fences barking at me, mostly in friendly fashion, and folks sitting on porches give me a friendly wave.

I see people through their windows settling into easy chairs and staring at television sets. Children laugh and giggle, making my trip worthwhile.

I like brick streets, so I always include one stretch which allows me to commiserate the history of my town, thinking of days gone by when horses clip-clopped along pulling buggies, wagons and surreys.

Invariably, I cut across the city park and nod at the teenagers who gather there.

If there's still light outside, I include a trek around the cemetery which is a real favorite of mine ... lots of familiar names welcome me to the eerie walking course, and I like to say their names as I pass by. I've given some of them nicknames and I always salute the graves of two old friends -- one a retired Army general and the other a captain.

Back to the streets, I meet the same walkers each evening as they make their rounds, some of them on five-mile treks, some rounding their block once or twice. We never stop and talk. We just nod and keep walking.

My favorite trick is to walk along kicking a small rock, usually a piece of gravel, and see how far I can go without losing it. Once I made it seven blocks with one rock -- my own little trophy.

There's one little stretch where I always break into a jog, but I don't stay with it very long. Going too fast might mean I would miss some snooping. And that's the favorite part of my evening.

I see squirrels and hear the birds. I pick up those dreadful styrofoam cups which midget-minded drivers toss out their windows. If it's campaign season, I take note of whose candidate signs are placed in specific yards. I try to figure out why those particular people might be backing a certain candidate. Usually I'm clueless.

I whistle softly as I walk and I often stumble slightly as I stare up at a star lit sky.

Then I turn the corner toward home and pick up some steam, sure to impress my wife that I've walked at a good clip.

I haven't figured out whether the walks are therapeutic or naughty. But whichever they are, I plan to hit the bricks again tonight.

Hometown neighbors put on too good a show to miss.

And it doesn't even require a ticket.

"Off the Cuff"

Looks like the sandlot boys were pretty good teachers after all

I stopped in the little town of Bartlett today and couldn't keep from taking a slow drive around town.

It didn't take long, but I found a place that reeked of naughty words, dreams of becoming a major league baseball player, and a small mountain of guilt.

Greg McRae was a playmate of mine who lived in Bartlett where his dad worked for the post office. Once or twice each summer, my mother would drop me off at Greg's house and we would spend our day on the playground at the school where we would put together a half dozen or so ball players for an afternoon of America's favorite sport.

All of us thought we were future shortstops, pitchers and fielders for the St. Louis Cardinals or some other big team. As far as I know, none of us ever made it. But then, I haven't seen the team for 45 years.

As we played ball, there was this voice that permeated the air. It sounded exactly like a little old lady.

Actually, it was a parrot. It perched in its cage which sat in a front window of a house located at the north edge of the ball field. It would scream, "Greg!" to my friend, and he would answer, "Shut up, bird!"

After listening to that predictable exchange for an entire morning, I came up with an idea: Teach the bird some new words.

I don't remember the little old lady's name who lived in the house, but I figured she wouldn't appreciate the type words I had in mind. So, our entire ragtag baseball team crept up to the window and sat below it for a good hour or two.

We said words that only big boys dared utter. The bird just sat there blinking his eyes. We thought we had failed. So we went home.

About a week later, my mother got a phone call from Greg's mother, and she was hot. She said the lady who lived by the school was accusing my friend Greg of teaching her parrot some new words. They were repulsive, nasty and vulgar. Or, so the lady thought.

Those words are today heard on television.

I remember the guilt I felt, but it seemed funny when I told the story to my buddies at home in Altamont. Greg's mom cut off my visits to her son, and I figured the bird forgot the pithy words we had taught it that afternoon.

But a year later, the bird was still hollering at kids on the playground and it sure wasn't saying, "Greg!" So, it had to be moved to an inside room where it reportedly never shut up. The little old lady lived out her life in ever-present earshot of that nasty little parrot.

As I sipped coffee at the Bartlett Coop before I left town this morning, I asked the waitress about the house and who lived in it now. She didn't know. But I got the idea from listening to the guys at the big table in the front window that they had gotten to know the bird quite well.

We must have been good teachers.

"Off the Cuff"

The cornbread is delicious and what's that yellow rock doing in our flower garden?

It was one of those romantic gestures that makes a man look good to his wife -- a promise to make supper.

She had put ham and beans in the crock pot that morning and they simmered throughout the day. Meanwhile, she was stuck at the newspaper office longer than I was, so I made the offer: "Hey, I'll go on home and make some cornbread to go with your beans."

"Oh, you don't need to do that," she said. "Just go up to the cafe and get two orders of waffle cornbread -- it's better than I can make anyway."

I didn't miss a stroke. "No way, Babe. Tonight will be special. If I can't follow the directions and make a pan of cornbread, there's something wrong with me."

She mumbled something about the time I made a mess in the kitchen trying to boil water, shrugged her shoulders and said, "Go for it. The church recipe book is above the stove."

I headed for home and dove into my personal challenge.

The first 20 minutes were spent searching for the church cookbook. So I called our daughter, Jenny, who lives at Independence.

"If you were standing in Kathy Taylor's kitchen, where would you find the church cookbook,?" I asked.

"Dad, if I know you, the cabinet doors are all open by now, so you're probably looking straight at it --- above the stove."

She was right.

"Thanks," I said. "I'm making cornbread for supper tonight."

She laughed. "Why don't you just call the cafe and get two orders to go?" she asked. "They'll have it ready in five minutes, and it's delicious."

I hung up in her ear.

Let's see, it looks like the recipe book is categorized by vegetables, desserts, casseroles and meats. So cornbread would fall into which category?

"Hello, Jenny? Sorry, we seem to have been cut off earlier. "In the church cookbook, where would you find ...."

"It's in the bread and cake section," she said. "I think it's on page thirty-two. But you're making a big mistake," she said.

Red faced and hurt, I slammed the phone down.

I was proud that I found the mixing bowl so I started reading the ingredients: Flour, cornmeal, baking powder, salt, sugar, milk and eggs.

My daughter recognized the number on her caller ID. She picked up the receiver and blurted, "Are you through pouting? What can't you find this time?"

Politely, I stammered, "If, if, if you were Kathy Taylor, wh-where would you keep your cornmeal?

"In the pantry, second shelf, round yellow box," she said before giving me the hangup treatment.

I made one more call to see what baking powder might look like, but it was too late -- I had already substituted something called baking soda.

There were 15 minutes of silence, then Jenny called me.

"Have you mixed everything together?" she asked?

"Yep, I mixed up everything," I replied, "but the recipe book says I should pour it into a greased pan -- like it's a liquid or something. What I'm looking at resembles a petrified, yellow, cow patty. It weighs about five pounds and has a wooden spoon stuck in the middle of the bowl."

There was silence on the other end. Then I heard laughter.

"Dad, I'm looking at the church recipe book that Mom gave me for my wedding. Are you sure you didn't get mixed up with the recipe right below it? I think you're making half cornbread and half doughnuts!"

Sure enough, my trifocal glasses had played tricks on me. I had added four cups of flour rather than one. I poured in a cup of sugar rather than one teaspoonful. And the nutmeg that I sprinkled on the top apparently gave it that foul smell.

"So, when will Mom be getting home?" Jenny asked.

"She's due in about 10 minutes," I sheepishly replied.

Then Jenny gave me an order: "Hang up the phone and go to the restaurant that's only three blocks from you. I'll call them to place your order. Don't say anything when you go pick it up -- otherwise you'll mess that up, too!"

Fifteen minutes later, we were sitting down to a bowl of homecooked ham and beans, waffle corn bread and Pepsi-Colas with lots of ice.

I said the blessing, then she gave me a pat on the hand.

"I'm a lucky woman," she said. "How many husbands know how to make cornbread and prepare a fine meal like this?"

I turned pink with embarrassment but never told her about the happenings a half hour earlier.

After supper, she walked over to the window and commented, "Has that yellowish rock always been in our flower garden?"

"Oh, that," I responded. "Well, it's a little gift that I picked up today at the nursery in Coffeyville."

She never changed her expression when she said so sweetly, "It's nice. I like it."

"Off the Cuff"

The sights and sounds of war rip the youth right out of them

A young soldier visited our home during the weekend and he left an indelible image in our hearts.

He was straight from the war in Iraq, so we tempered our questions and comments, wanting him to relax and enjoy the company of old friends.

While the young Army private sat in our front room, my mind rushed back a half century to the days when soldiers were freshly back from the war in Europe, the Pacific and Korea. Those soldiers and sailors were so old, so mature, so ready to head into adulthood.

Or so I thought, as a little boy.

In reality they were the same age as the boy who sat in our front room last weekend, calling everyone ma'am and sir, and fidgeting as we asked polite questions.

Could he possibly be a member of the famous 101st Airborne Division? Of course the answer was yes, and he returned home as a man, just as those guys did back in the late 1940s and early '50s.

I also remember the men and women of my own generation who went to a place called Vietnam -- how they came home with a distant stare in their eyes that remains there, even today. It was 25 years later before most of them talked much about the war, and even then only if when in the presence of another "Nam" vet.

My wife and I went to bed at the usual time, leaving the

young soldier to visit with our daughter and her husband, who happens to be the soldier's brother. The next morning, Jenny relayed many of his stories, and undoubtedly she kept some of them in her heart. For a few hours he had someone his age who would listen, laugh with him, and help him catch up on the good life here in the U.S.A.

After seeing snapshots of his living accommodations in Iraq and the parched landscape of that war-torn country, it was no wonder that he spent most of his time gazing around our living room and slumping down in the comfy recliner.

I recall those returning from the '40s and '50s wars enjoying the simple routines of playing basketball or doing farm chores, almost like they craved such common goings-on.

Letting this young soldier enjoy some quiet conversation while sipping on a Pepsi poured over crush ice and eating nachos was our only offer to his rest and relaxation.

He now goes back for more training, then has every intention of returning to Iraq where fighting for freedom is, seemingly, a never ending job.

And there is no doubt that he is a man. We could tell by the distant stare in his eyes.

CHAPTER SIX

The big book arrives

A small-town newspaper editor walks a delicate balance, misunderstood by most, appreciated for his influence, yet ribbed for his supposedly partisan editorial stands.

In reality he takes few such stands. It just seems that way when the newspaper tries to explain issues in such a way that both sides are understood.

Still, at the end of the day, he holds his head high on that five-block walk home. There is a sense of history-making among folks who publish newspapers. A weekly newspaper is truly a chronicle of what happened the previous week and a promotion of what is on the distant horizon.

It is only at year's end that the Chronicle looks like a history book because that is when the postmaster leaves a card in the mail box saying, "Large Book — C.O.D."

That means the bound file for the past year has arrived from a place in Wisconsin where the Chronicle sends a complimentary newspaper each week. When all 52 issues in a year are compiled they are assembled, placed in a hardback cover and bound, and on the front of the book, the name of the newspaper and the year are printed in gold letters.

It's amazing how much better the news stories read after a few months go by. Same with the columns and editorials. The hometown Chronicle looks pretty impressive when dressed up in such regal fashion.

"I wish everybody in town could see this," his wife says quietly as her eyes scan the pages. "If they only knew that we printed 824 pages last year."

It never feels like history writing when a particular edition is being put to bed. Fact is, the editor is never happy with an edition. There is so much more out there to report. But since the amount of advertising determines the number of pages, he must settle for printing the obvious, and seldom the stories that are mischievous or investigative in nature.

A newspaperman also deals with facts, not rumor, so there's a lot that goes unreported. Readers often are disturbed when the editor shrugs off a rumor they've heard. "Where did you get your information?" is always his first question.

"I heard it at the cafe," comes the reply. "Check it out for yourself."

"So, I should ask the cafe, right?"

The reader feels put down and the editor knows he did it again -- assuming everyone knows that rumors do not make the news columns.

He gets his thrills, and gains a creative catharsis from writing pithy editorials and punchy columns, most of which don't amount to anything. He knows, however, that the opinion page of the Chronicle is well read.

"I don't know why I'm re-upping this paper," an elderly gent will say as he pays his subscription. "The wife likes to read all the gossip, but I don't care a thing about it."

Then he will take 10 minutes of the front-office clerk's time to tell his side of issues he has perused on the op-ed page.

He reads the Chronicle.

So does his family. Neighbors, too. The hometown Chronicle is kept in the house for an entire week, then admittedly, the garbage is wrapped in it. But many country weeklies are passed from neighbor to neighbor -- a habit that newspaper owners don't know how to take. They appreciate the paper being so popular that it is passed along to someone else, yet they wish everyone would buy their own newspaper. Darn it.

He is interrupted by a good friend who sticks his head in the front door of the office. "Hey, Scoop! I just heard the football coach is quitting after this season. Check it out!"

"Where'd you hear it?"

"Down at the ball field."

The editor smirks. "Let's see, I should interview the football field ...."

Oh, no. He did it again.

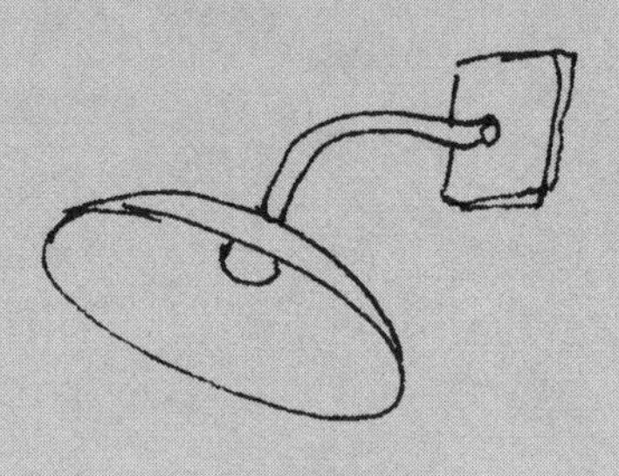

"Off the Cuff"

There are engineers, auctioneers and it's pertineer springtime in Kansas

I love the differences between the small towns where our newspapers are located.

It's a tiny corner of southeast Kansas, and the towns are fiercely competitive. Ancient sports rivalries keep the communities at arm's length from the others.

That's aggravating when a newspaper is trying its best to survive by pulling towns together for economic growth and social survival, but there's also something beautiful about the differences between these towns.

They all have their unique way of talking, and that's where I like to pull up a chair in the local coffee shop, listen and appreciate the local chatter. It's not that they are backward -- far from it. They travel all over the place, visiting and doing business in surrounding towns. The towns have names like Chetopa, Burden, Atlanta, Oswego, Altamont, Edna, Oswego, Moline, Caney, Cherryvale, Sedan, Howard, Beaumont, Longton and Grenola. They're wonderful places full of delightful people.

A Chetopa reader came to our office this week and said, "I couldn't get along without my *Ad*vance." Oh, I like that. Emphasis upon the "ad" is pure sweetness to a newspaperman.

In our Sedan office we have lots of readers who pay their subscriptions by the year but pick up their papers at the office.

One lovely woman sticks her head in the door, grabs two

papers and hollers, “Adaolita!”

I was startled by the yodel-sounding word at first, but I noticed she invariably was answered by an “OK, thanks!” from our staffers who were busy mailing newspapers.

Then I learned the trick. Break it down and it’s “Ada and Olita” whose papers are being picked up. You’ve got to be a native to understand stuff like that.

Our Oswego editor called this morning to tell me, “I’m doing a story on Odanadaag.”

Upon inquiring further, my ears heard it right -- “Odin the dog.”

It was about the a local police dog that’s been added to the squad.

A Southern gentleman had moved to Caney several years ago and he called the newspaper office to place a classified ad. He drawled as he dictated the words: Wanted - pasture for ten thousand calves.

Startled, I repeated the ad back to him: Pasture for ten thousand calves?

That’s right he said, and our paper went to press with the ad.

That night, our phone rang at home.

“Where did you get that stuff about ten thousand calves,” came his friendly drawl. “I just need a little pasture for my ten cows and calves!”

We didn’t charge him for the ad.

I haven’t figured out yet whether there’s a “howl” in Hallowell or a “hall,” and I don’t understand why an Altamont mama objected to her daughter being called a Grizzly. “She’s a member of the Lady Grizzlies,” the lady explained, “but she’s not grizzly.”

Go figure.

Over at Cherryvale, their athletic teams once were called the Fighting Cherries. Naughty minds converted them to the Chargers.

See? It was so spirited before. Now it's plain vanilla, but admittedly, supercharged!

In Altamont they say "crick" but in Caney it's "creek."

At Tyro it's "nick" but in nearby Dearing it's a "neck."

At one county fair they call girl sheep "yoes" but in the adjoining county they're "ewes" (yooze).

And, if I drive ten miles into Oklahoma, it's a whole different world. If they say "stick" it has at least three syllables. I'm good at adjusting my lingo to the place where I stop for coffee.

I can sip coffee with the ranchers at the Woodshed in Edna and hear every accent from German to Okie to Yankee.

It's my favorite part of the week when I can partake of that communion, even though I'd be embarrassed for my buddies to know that I'm analyzing their speech patterns.

At P&J's in Howard, friends greet me with "Howdy."

At the Green Door and Ranch Cafe in Sedan they say, "Hidee."

Friends at the Caney Kitchen say, "Snew-thew?"

And, at the Buckboard in Chetopa, it's always, "Cha-know?"

I like them all. But seldom does anybody utter my favorite word: Pertineer.

I grew up with it and refuse to remove it from my vocabulary.

After all, it's pertineer springtime.

"Off the Cuff"

A creaking wagon, a dog named Mike, and a pioneer family full of hope

In my work as a country publisher, I drive from town to town, especially now that we publish seven weekly newspapers. As I drive, I see things which bring back stories of old.

One of them involves the autumn, and a story my grandmother told me many times. Although she is long gone, and would have been 123 years old if still living today, I well remember her quiet tale of the covered wagon which brought her from Illinois to Missouri, through southeast Kansas and into the small Indian Territory community of Timber Hill where I was born -- just south of Chetopa, Kansas.

It was in the late 1880s when her father and mother loaded up their kids, all their furniture, ample supplies, and a rosebush in a gunny sack, and headed toward Kansas where my great-grandfather heard there were jobs in the mines.

Tied to the back of the wagon was a milk cow, and trailing far and wide was a dog named Mike.

When they arrived in Kansas, it was quickly learned that jobs were scarce, even though the coal mines and granite quarries were doing land-office business. That's when someone told my great-grandfather about the small mines being started near Bluejacket, just over the line in Indian Territory.

So, they headed out again, staying the night at Baxter Springs, then traveling west to Chetopa where they camped out before fording the Neosho River just east of town. From there they turned south, crossed Russell Creek and found their way to Timber Hill.

My grandmother was only six at the time, and it was only nine years later that she married a coal miner named Spike Walker --- my grandfather. And the rest is history. Remnants of that family still live throughout this area to this day.

Grandma would stare off into the heavens as she retold her story: The covered wagon was so full that the kids had to be "stuffed" into holes beneath the table, trunks and wooden boxes in the wagon bed. Since it was late fall, my great-grandfather was anxious to conclude the trip before winter set in, and he was nervous about crossing the Neosho which he had heard was wide and sometimes treacherous.

Arriving at Chetopa, they found the river to be low and shallow, and the crossing was made with the help of local men who guided them across with long ropes, pulling with another team of horses on the west bank.

Grandma told of the fun which the children enjoyed along the way. Since the wagon ride was so bumpy, the children walked much of the way, playing as they went. "The kids would run far ahead of the wagon," she would relate. "Once we got way ahead of the wagon, we'd sit down in the middle of the road and play as fast as we could, then watch as the wagon slowly passed by, and kept playing until we could hardly see it anymore. Then just before it disappeared in the distance, we'd all jump up and run really fast to catch it, pass it by again, and run ahead a safe distance -- and there we would sit down and play again."

Her father, who had a Quaker background, made the children listen each night as he read from the Bible, and all the kids were required to read scripture passages as their only source of schooling while en route to their new home. Once they arrived there, they discovered a community with no school, so my great-grandfather helped to build one. Today, only remnants of the Timber Hill School remain --- a ghostly reminder of the day more than 120 years ago when this special family arrived to plant their roots in local soil.

Today, I often drive out to the Neosho River bridge and stare across the water. I love to imagine how thrilling, albeit difficult, those times must have been as a family lumbered all the way across Missouri, cutting through the corner of southeast Kansas, and found its way into Indian Territory to start a new life.

Autumn stirs such precious memories.

And, yes, the rosebush still blooms in our backyard.

"Off the Cuff"

You don't have to be old to enjoy the songs of yesteryear

The radio in our office was playing softly when a young female worker commented, "I like that song. What is it?"

It was Johnny Mathis singing his classic song, "The Twelfth of Never," and the seemingly ageless singer recorded it in 1957.

I have to admit that the first button on my pickup radio is programmed to a golden oldie station. The songs of the '50s and '60s take me back to a simpler time when music wasn't so harsh and singers were far from the likes of Michael Jackson, Eminem or Shania Twain.

So it made my day to hear a girl barely out of her teens reaching for the volume knob so she could get a better listen on Johnny Mathis.

When that song first came out, the radios looked different than they look today. We listened to our local radio station but also loved Dick Diondi who could be picked up late at night on WLS in Chicago. KOMA in Oklahoma City was a full channel AM station that could be heard from coast to coast and it was our mainstay.

Today, the oldie songs emanate from area stations that subscribe to Westwood One and other national services. They are computer driven, finely tuned and tightly cued from song to song. In the old days, it was fast talking disc jockeys in our small Kansas towns who kept the vinyl platters spinning.

The funny thing is: When you get my age, the term golden

oldie is widely defined, meaning everything from the big band sounds of the '40s to Elvis in the 1950s to the Beatles of the 1960s to Three Dog Night in the '70s to the Eagles of the 1980s.

It's a big list, and the rules go something like this: If the song is more than 10 years old and you're over 25, you have your own list of golden oldies. They don't have to be smooth as silk or corny as Kelloggs or slow as the seven-year itch. Oldies create reminiscent thoughts that are somehow attached to your radio knob -- the one that switches on the sounds that take you back to the moments you experienced with the music of yesteryear.

As I drive my pickup from town to town, I switch from these smooth classics to country music to classical to contemporary Christian -- and each one has its own version of golden oldies.

There is something comforting to a person who once sang along with a special song on the radio, only to hear it many years later being replayed for a younger audience.

Musical tastes change. So do musicians. But the music stays the same. It's the listener who turns a bit more golden each year, and it's the memories accompanying the old tunes that makes everyone, regardless of age, apt to turn up the volume when a golden oldie hits the air.

" *... until the twelfth of never, and that's a long, long time.*"

Just ask Johnny Mathis about that. He's still recording today.

"Off the Cuff"

Doesn't every little boy take a bath in glycerin and rose water?

Springtime, to this ol' newspaperman, means losing a few pounds (I'll start tomorrow), getting tanned, tuning up the lawn mower, and shedding a layer of skin.

Yes, dear readers, you heard it right -- I look forward to spring because I'm part snake. My skin gets really dry and scruffy during the wintertime, then smooths up each April. My wife calls it "the shedding season." I call it embarrassing.

When I sit down in a chair and cross one foot over my knee, I habitually brush the scruff off my dark socks. It looks like dandruff, but it's too far from my bald head to bear that name. The same goes for my heels, elbows and that unreachable space between the wings on my back. Yep, for six months out of the year, I have itchy wings. Match that, Victor Murdock!

When I was a little boy, my mother took me to a doctor in an upstairs office in a nearby city. He probed, beamed a flashlight in my eyes, rubbed my skin and pronounced, "He's allergic to strawberries."

It made me mad. Mom, too. She slammed down the two dollar fee and stormed out with me in tow.

Over the years, every doctor or nurse who has ever taken my blood pressure has asked, "What's the matter with your skin?"

I figure they should tell me, but so far, nobody has ever diagnosed anything other than wintertime rough skin.

In grade school, I would entertain the kids in my country school by striking a match across my knuckles. I was so very cool.

In junior high, my buddies called me "Alligator," and the basketball coach labeled me "Slick" because I always greased myself with lotion after donning my uniform.

Before we got married, Kathy didn't dream of steamy bedroom scenes after the wedding. All she could think about was taking a wire brush to my legs and back. She tried, but to no avail.

Just last night, she came in the door with her newest version of a wire brush -- a jar of sugar scrub. "Just take a shower then rub this stuff all over then wash it off," she said.

I sugared myself until I was sweet, but the scruffs returned by morning.

I've soaked in hot tubs. I've tried every conceivable vitamin. I've inhaled the fumes of simmering papyrus. I've walked in the rain, drank pure mineral oil and sung in a hot shower for hours on end.

My mother always poured glycerin and rose water in the bathtub for me, and when I left for college she bought me a gallon jug of Vaseline skin lotion.

I've tried coconut cream and goat's milk potions. Somebody sent me a jar of Blue Stuff which cured my hurts but left my scales intact.

My dermis seems to worry other people more than it bothers me. After all, I know that springtime will bring relief. So, starting in February, I start seeing the light at the end of the tunnel.

I look forward to April and May because it's scale shedding time.

It's a seasonal ritual that's religiously observed by snakes, alligators and newspapermen who itch between our wings.

CHAPTER SEVEN

Temperatures and bank accounts get mighty cool during January

There are no credentials for being a journalist and sometimes that works to the dismay of the weekly editor.

Folks assume that those who work in a weekly newspaper office never quite made it to the daily newsroom. Nothing could be further from the truth.

Chronicle writers follow the same reporting styles, page layout methods and news gathering ethics as journalists follow at the *New York Times*.

A weekly editor usually owns his own newspaper. He or she likes the freedom allowed by ownership, even though the financial rewards seldom rise to the level of those enjoyed by a daily newspaper editor or publisher.

It has always irked the Chronicle editor when people refer to his newspaper as little. He knows that every word printed in the Chronicle contains news about the hometown where the newspaper is published. That's not the case with daily newspapers in the same area -- those bastions of information that carry mostly national news from the Associated Press, all of which was heard or watched on CNN the day before.

While the number of pages may only be 10 or 12, the Chronicle staff considers it to be a mammoth edition, because news and pictures printed in a weekly newspaper cannot be found any place else on earth. That makes any local editor a true historian. Every word in every edition is unique, therefore big.

It is a family of journalists who write for the hometown

Chronicle. A true family. There are employees who take pictures, sell ads and write news, too, but the sentiments behind the publishing of this weekly newspaper are etched deeply into the ink-stained emotions of a mom and dad, son and daughter, any of whom could have spent their careers in some distant newsroom of a daily newspaper but chose life in a weekly newspaper instead.

Still, when it's January and local advertisers seem cooler than the frigid temperatures outside, the Chronicle editor makes the same comparisons to the big-time -- and feels little.

He gets noticeably quiet during the first three months of each year, carrying financial stress on his face, yet holding to the advice given to him on the day he bought the newspaper nearly 40 years before:

When it comes January and February, just hold on and don't give up. The sun always shines again.

Even though the fig shall not blossom, neither shall the grapes bloom in the vines nor olives grow from the trees. Even though the fields bear no harvest and the flock be cut off from the fold, and even when there shall be no herd in the stalls, yet I will rejoice in the Lord, I will joy in the God of my salvation. The Lord God is my strength.

Habakkuk 3:17-19

"Off the Cuff"

Time is not for watching, it is for enjoying and savoring

My kids chipped in a bought me a new watch for Christmas -- a really nice one.

I also got a desk radio with a clock in it.

So, with time literally on my hands through the holidays, I made a quick count of the watches and clocks in our home.

I counted nine clocks in the house and that didn't include the TV sets and computers which have digital readouts of the time. We have at least four wristwatches and a pocketwatch. There's a grandfather clock and a pendulum clock in the living room. The cookstove and microwave oven include clocks.

Of course, each of our cars has a digital clock on the dashboard.

At our office, there are clocks everywhere.

Our answering machines tell us when calls come in; our computers tell us when e-mails were sent; our bedside alarms coax us into each new day.

The last thing we do before going to bed at night is glance at the clock, then at first light it's our first view of the day.

We are filling out our planners; creating time slots for our ballgames, meetings, work routines, crop planting. Heck, even the romantic habits of our livestock are given "times" on the clock and calendar.

In such a world, where clocks, time pieces and time schedules are paramount to our very existence, I simply must revert back to when our home had only one clock. And, somehow, it seemed that we had more time back then.

Our clock was a simple wind-up model that sat on the kitchen counter. The stove had no clock -- we didn't have electricity. We had no fancy grandfather clocks or answering machines telling us when somebody called. We didn't have a telephone.

Our car had a heater. Period.

We kept time mostly by the meals which Mom served: Six, twelve and six, every day.

A couple hours after supper was over we went to bed and nobody ever woke up in the middle of the night and glanced at the bedside clock. We had none.

My point is: We live in a society that is obsessed with time. And, it's just possible that keeping track of the time, glancing at clocks and watches a hundred times a day and night, checking the TV channels to see if it's "time" for favorite programs, and driving our cars lickety-split in order to "beat the clock" has made us into a time driven, fidgety, overly anxious bunch of ants, all bound up over how much time we have left in our day, or night, or job, or trip ... or life.

I have a feeling that removing television sets would do the most to improve life in our homes. And second, I would throw out all but one clock in each dwelling.

Each of us has 24 hours in each day to live. Perhaps if we spent less effort trying to harness our time, or adjust it, read it, manage it, and catch up with it -- we might just find the handle on better relationships with those with whom we spend our time.

If we eat only when we're hungry, go to bed when we get

sleepy, get up when the sun shines through the window, expect people to answer their phones only when somebody is there to say hello, leave a little earlier when we go someplace, cook our food until it's done, watch TV when we have absolutely nothing else to do and put ourselves into our work, school and play in such a way that clock-watching never occurs to us, then we might find the key to peering into the new year and looking forward to every minute, every hour and every day of that idyllic place we call "tomorrow."

We've got the time, if we just do it.

"Off the Cuff"

Raw rumpery could be the dirge of all our evil ways

The sermon in a local church last Sunday revealed a fascinating story from the book of I Samuel in the *Old Testament.*

It involved the Ark of the Covenant being stolen from the Israelites by the infamous Philistines. It seems God zapped the Philistines with the plagues of the wilderness for their deeds — including one which could be of use in today's society.

Super-hemorrhoids.

God gave a plague of hemorrhoids to everybody who had a part in stealing the Ark of the Covenant, or even those who spoke of the crime.

Talk about cutting down on gossip -- that punishment definitely would do the trick.

Maybe we spoiled Americans would act and talk differently if we knew that hemorrhoids, immediate and painful, would be our reward for verbally destroying that which is good.

Perhaps, just perhaps, we'd see the following:

• The Democrats and Republicans would sit down together and rationally discuss the future of our country. Either that, or they wouldn't sit at all!

• Husbands and fathers might stay at home more, play with their kids, talk softly and lovingly to their wives.

• Screenwriters and TV entertainers might think twice before writing trashy scripts that are filled with sacrilege.

• Coffee shops would abound with happy campers.

• The Bulls would bench Dennis Rodman where he'd spend every second of every game sitting on a rubber doughnut.

• The messages on t-shirts, bumper stickers and pasture signs would be nicer, smarter.

• Clerks would care, customers would be grateful, and bosses would be thoughtful.

• Rush Limbaugh wouldn't change at all -- he'd still be a pain in the rear.

You get the idea — God had a great way of protecting His Glory in those old days. But of course, He had a better way in mind, and we're glad He did. But it never hurts to re-read the letters of biblical history just to be reminded that God does wield a stern hand when He needs it, and a sense of humor as well.

And as for smart aleck editors who write silly columns about serious subjects ... too-o-o-o late.

The plague has already hit with full force.

Scoot over, Rush. Hand me a doughnut, Michael Jackson ... sir, or madam, as the case may be.

"Off the Cuff"

A man never wins the thermostat battle

They call it marital bliss.

I've had plenty of it over the past 34 years. Wouldn't trade Kathy for anything or anyone in the world.

But if you ever hear that ol' Rudy has gone south on his bride, the reason will be summed up in two words -- *the thermostat.*

Yep, I know that's not grounds for anything, but by golly, the two women in my house -- Kathy and our 18-year-old daughter Jenny -- are about to freeze me out. And I'm getting (brrrr!) sick of it.

I don't know why the Good Lord created these two women with built-in heaters, and gave me an open door to the ice box, but it happened. All they have to do is comb their hair, make a bed, or answer a phone, and -- whammo! They're boiling hot.

Meanwhile, yours truly is wearing two layers of shirts and usually looking for a cozy sweatshirt to go over it all. I haven't been warm in 20 years.

Then I go to work in Oswego, and there's another one (who shall remain nameless). She, too, cranks down the thermostat as soon as she enters the front door of our office, and my blood starts to curdle, just from sheer freezing. Therefore, I'm cold every minute of every day.

So I'm wondering: Am I the only guy in Kansas who hasn't thawed out of winter yet? Is there another male out there who shivers from the moment he wakes up in the morning until his head hits the pillow at night?

I truly feel that the females in my life are guilty of harassment; that they have no compassion for a man who works hard, keeps the ol' team together, fights wars (OK, so I did my fighting on a college campus in the 1960s), and must subject himself to such trauma as hernia tests and prostate exams. One would think one might get an ounce of respect.

But, n-e-e-w-w-w-w-w-w.

Here's the way it usually goes.

I walk in our back door, give everyone a cheerful greeting, and I notice that icicles have started to form on the cabinet doors. So I quietly tip-toe down the hallway and turn the thermostat to 85 -- right where thermostats belong, right?

I then change clothes and sit down to watch the evening news on TV, only to find myself asleep within two seconds. Then, not 15 minutes later, I am awakened by the sting of frostbite and the sound of gritching.

It goes something like this: *If-you-wanta-get-warm-why-don't-you-put-on-a-coat?* That's usually followed by a smirky comment from the other one: *You-could-always-try-cooking-supper-and-cleaning-like-we-are-doing!* Boy, that one always hurts, especially after all I've done to keep America free and our family from falling into communist hands. And did I mention the prostate thing?

So this last Christmas everyone in the family chipped in and bought me an electric blanket, and it has created new, romantic feelings in my life. Oh, not for Kathy, mind you -- but for that beautiful, warm blanket! I find myself going to bed early so I can snuggle and growl. Kathy and Jenny like that because the sounds they're accustomed to hearing are grumbling and teeth chattering.

Here it is the middle of March and they've already been running the air conditioner for a month. Meanwhile, I'm eating meals while wearing gloves and a muffler wrapped around my neck, with a sock cap pulled down over my ears.

It's quite a sight, this harassment that occurs at our house every night. But I shall endure. It is yet another battle in the rough-and-tumble world of an abused American male.

Still, I live with hope. Come springtime, when the sunshine starts thawing my toes, and the ground starts to sprout impatiens and vincas -- I plan to take off one layer of shirts and give Jack Frost a chance to rest for several months.

But when I go to bed at night, my new blankie will still be there, waiting to be turned on, coddled with flirty words and tucked underneath my chin as I fall off to sleep.

And for a few hours, at least -- an old veteran of life's great wars will finally get some rest.

The marriage will survive.

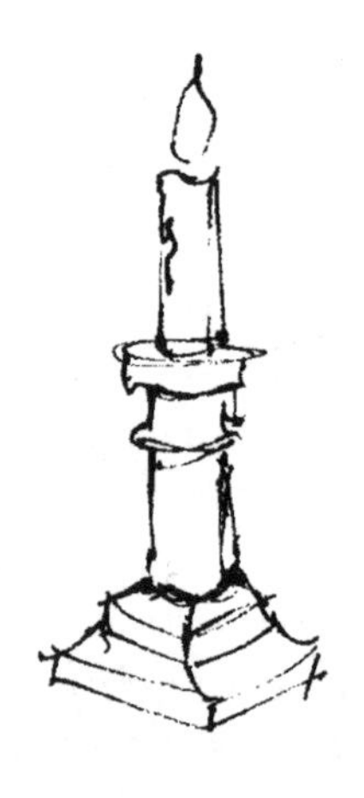

Cramming nine bags on one arm shouldn't be expected of a man

Older folks like to tell their children how many sacks of groceries they once bought with a five dollar bill.

Modern-day conversation with our children (all adults) revolves around another subject: "How many plastic bags can you carry from your car at the same time?"

Our daughter, who totes around a handsome little 10-month-old boy, finds it is important to make one trip from the car after a trip to the grocery store. She simply can't take a chance on leaving him unattended inside the house while she darts back and forth to the car.

So her record is nine bags. That's right: nine bags that she places on her arms then scoots them up past her elbows almost to her shoulders. She places the heaviest ones on first, leaving the bread and eggs for last. Remember, that's all on one arm. The other one is reserved for the little tike who predictably grabs the bags and tries to rip them apart before she gets to the kitchen.

Usually one or two bags drop to the driveway, at which point she turns cutely red and scolds the little one, emphasizing his middle name as she tells him off. At that, he touches her face, tweaks her nose then lays his head on her shoulder.

She drops the red face and goes only with the "cute," and life is good.

I remember my mother making trips to the country store near our farm and returning home with only one or two paper sacks.

That was because we raised most of our own food, from beef to beets, chicken to corn, tomatoes to home churned butter.

The store "carried a ticket" for us, meaning we had a charge account, and once a month my dad would load up the kids and head to the store to pay the tab. It was our favorite day of the month because Mr. Farmer (yes, that was his name) would give each child a free ice cream cone anytime a grocery bill was paid in full.

So you can understand the crinkle on my brow as a young adult in my family says, "I carried nine sacks of stuff on one arm."

I remember old-time paper sacks being heavier than those of today. Of course, few customers today even want paper. They can't carry more than three paper sacks, while young people like our daughter can cram nine sacks on one arm.

Today, our society is more convenience oriented than prudent buyers of groceries. We leave the office at 5:30, run by the store to pick up a few items for supper, then head home. Or we'll stop by the local hamburger drive-in or pizza store and take a more expensive but less hectic route.

They don't have charge accounts at those places, so there's no ice cream cone at month's end.

So far, I haven't found the need to thread nine or ten sacks of groceries on my arm. But then, I don't buy groceries either. Every time my wife sends me to the store, I come back with stuff she didn't order and I seldom bring home the specific item she wanted in the first place.

That's why men look to females for grocery-buying and plastic sack-cramming. Sure, it's sexist to say that, but the way I talk with my hands and arms, I'd probably sling a ham over the neighbor's fence anyway.

It's safer to allow a woman to line her arms with plastic sacks.

One word of caution: When she finally gets inside the kitchen door, leave her alone for at least five minutes.

Women still have this crazy expectation that the men in their lives might lend a hand, and it takes a few minutes of fuming before they realize, again, how one-sided life really is.

"Off the Cuff"

Every editor experiences a high when the big press starts rolling

Watching a newspaper as it comes off the press is not unlike a wino who searches the gutters for coins to buy his next quart.

It is downright intoxicating for an editor as he stands in the noisy pressroom after a week of chasing news stories, ads and pictures to fill his edition.

The aroma of newsprint, especially on modern-day offset presses, smells a bit like a dirty diaper, yet the prospect of excitement lures him into the fray each time the hometown paper starts meandering through the rollers, into the folder and onto the conveyor belt where papers are retrieved and bundled.

The pages flip by at dizzying speed and the editor prays that he caught all the typos before sending the edition to press. He holds the inky pages in his hand while catching the eye of the pressman. "The front page picture is too dark," he will say, much to the press operator's chagrin. But the adjustment is made anyway.

Then, after a couple minutes of looking it over, he gives a thumbs up, tosses the paper in the trash barrel and walks out. The next edition awaits him and he will spend little time admiring or groaning over today's printed product.

That's the way it is with editors, always running toward tomorrow, taking precious little time for today and trying like crazy to forget their yesterdays.

"Off the Cuff"

Because of a special teacher over 50 years ago, I know who I am today

While packing away our Christmas decorations last weekend, I reacquainted myself with a relic of the past as I made trips to the attic.

The relic is a small metal box, once used to hold 3x5 cards, and I stumble across it every few years. Inside it are scribbled notes and junky little keepsakes. It holds many memories for me.

But the box itself is worth keeping because it reminds me of a very special lady in my life — one who died only five years ago. Her name was Irene Nevins and for many years she held down the southwest corner room at Altamont Grade School where I was fortunate enough to sit in her fourth grade class.

She was the best teacher I ever had and I suspect many other former fourth graders at Altamont will avow the same. The reason is quite simple: She taught us who we were.

* * *

On the inside of Mrs. Nevins' classroom, to the left of the door, hung a round mirror. Above it were written these words: "Know who you are."

That mirror got a lot of use:

• When a girl was caught passing a note to a friend during class, she was sent to the mirror and told to take a good look -- 30 minutes worth of looking!

• A nasty boy who burped out loud also spent some time at the mirror. And, there was the usual lecture from Mrs. Nevins: "Take a good look at yourself, young man," she would say. "Is that really who you want to be?"

• A standing rule for class members was to walk in front of that mirror and glance in it as we exited the room -- every time. The words, "Know who you are," became indelibly etched in our minds.

Over the years since that 1955 class, there have been lots of times that I have lost track of who I am -- but only temporarily. That's because Irene Nevins taught me well in her not-always-so-lovely way that the guy in the mirror is the fellow who causes most of my misdeeds and holds the answer to correcting every one of them.

Some 20 years ago I was to interview for a position in Topeka where I was promised a bright future working for the State of Kansas.

As I walked to the front door of the Docking State Office Building, I glanced toward the huge glass window which was adjacent to the sidewalk and saw myself trudging toward an uncertain future.

I didn't know the man I saw in the reflection. It wasn't me.

I paused to think about Mrs. Nevins' mirror that windy day in Topeka, and inwardly repeated those words: "Know who you are."

I canceled the interview and headed back to my little newspaper office in southeast Kansas, double-timing it all the way. I may not be happy with the shape of the guy I see in the window-glass reflection, but I sure do recognize him.

At the end of our fourth grade year, Mrs. Nevins lined up

the kids and presented each of us with two gifts: One was a small, round mirror. The other was a little green file-box --- a perfect place to keep life's little secrets.

My wife knows that nobody had better throw away that little box. In fact, I moved it to a shelf in my office today. It needs no inscription nor embellishment for it is merely a reminder that once I was taught by a lovely lady who made me stare at myself when I was alone, troubled, naughty or just downright ornery.

And because of Irene Nevins, I know who I am.

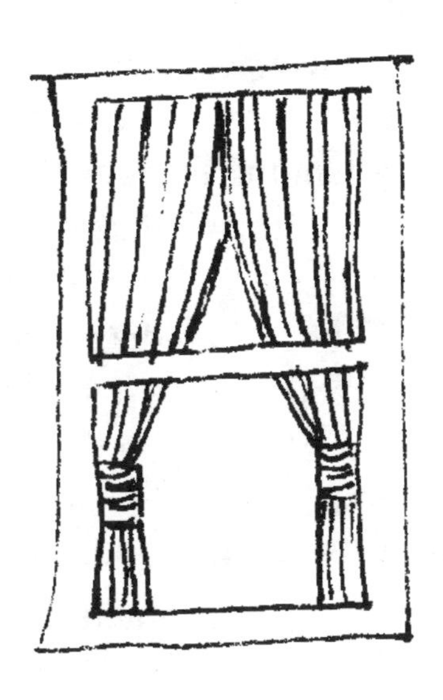

"Off the Cuff"

Nothing unites rural America like the arrival of summer fairs

It's summertime in Kansas, and that means one thing to a newspaper family: County fairs.

My wife asked me last night, "Well, which county fair is next?"

I sat there for a good five minutes and didn't answer, because it wasn't an easy question to answer. There are at least eight area fairs that our little newspapers cover.

We're fair minded. It's a malady that we like, mostly because of what it does to the towns we like so much.

The opening of a local fair is always a thrilling event for folks who live in that community. And it has special meaning to those who grew up attending this yearly gathering of young people, parents and all the organizations who are intertwined in it.

A fair is so much more than demonstrations, exhibits, livestock shows, rodeos and a big ferris wheel. It is the culmination of a full year of planning and work by folks who are neighbors and good friends. It brings everyone closer together and gives us a chance to catch up on friendships which, because of busy schedules, get scooted to the back shelf where they gather dust.

Then, late in July each year, farmer families head to town with trailers hooked to the back of their pickups, 4-H members put the finishing touches on their projects, local entertainers pick out some new songs, campers start setting up adjacent to the fairgrounds, fair board members add one more coat of paint to a building or repair one more fence, the northeast part of town starts to sound like a big barnyard and a row of carnival trucks file through town heading toward the fairgrounds.

Merchants stock up on the stuff they know will sell during this special week and the hometown newspaper crams ads, stories, lists, schedules and pictures into a special fair edition.

Then the big day arrives.

Farm kids groom their lambs, calves, cows, hogs and horses. They set up lawn chairs and sleeping bags in the livestock barns, trying their best to be in the direct path of the giant fans that blow summer air through the barns.

The aroma of barbecue, hamburgers, popcorn and other foods permeate the air and the humidity automatically jumps to 99 percent -- just because it's fair week.

Farmers stand around and talk, shaking their heads at the low prices on wheat and corn. Cattlemen compare notes on where their neighbor bought that bull, or which auction barn is pulling the best prices.

Homemakers admire each other's projects and tell stories about "back when" some well-known grandmother consistently won the cherry pie contest.

Little boys wear boots and cowboy hats. Girls don't look much different, although their jeans seem to have a bit more fashion to them. But the two genders never have any trouble knowing the difference -- the county fair is a great time for romantic glances, walks to the park and a few secret rendezvous.

By week's end, everyone will be anxious to return home -- all tired and needing a good, hot shower. Even those who go home every night find the week to be an exhausting one.

Still, memories are made at the fairgrounds, and the tired bones soon will be forgotten, replaced by chatter about next year and "we'd better get started right now."

Nothing in rural America pulls families together more than a fair. Nothing energizes a small town more than hosting one. Nothing makes children have more productive fun than a week spent at the fair.

Nothing makes a small town more beautiful than having hundreds, hopefully thousands, of people converging on one little piece of real estate to enjoy the hallmark of all the year's events -- the summer fair.

Could be the best-kept secret in America, and quite frankly, we'd like to keep it that way. Big-city ways and worries haven't invaded these fairs yet.

Shhhhh.

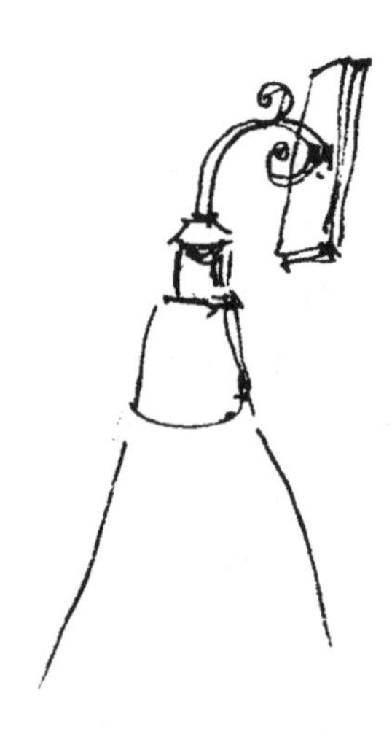

CHAPTER EIGHT

Letting the pesky telephone ring would calm the editor's stress

A simple telephone is the editor's nemesis.

Even when he was young, the Chronicle editor insisted that someone else answer this bothersome, noisy instrument. Invariably, he would get trapped when he picked up a jingling telephone.

One time he added up all the hours he had spent on the phone during his newspaper career and it came to something like eight years.

When he first bought the newspaper in 1970, there was only one phone in the whole office. It was black and inky and hung on the wall beside his desk.

Then progress set in.

Before long, there were extensions to the back offices and two lines added. That meant every time it rang, at least three people hollered, "I'll get it!"

It bothered him that he was paying three people to drop everything and rush for the phone.

Still, the telephone offered his closest link to society, because editors aren't known for mingling too tightly with the world outside.

Most editors and publishers are basically shy, but it doesn't come out that way. They are viewed as elitist and nerdy and folks like to ridicule them. So a ringing telephone at the Chronicle office often goes unanswered if he's the only one working.

While he probably knows as much about the goings-on of the world all around him as anybody in town, able to grasp details dating back to the founding of the town in 1869, he never knows the price of a want ad and seldom remembers names of old ladies who stop by to pay their subscriptions.

He will grouse at a county commissioner for raising taxes by a half mill, able to cite line items in the budget that could be cut. Yet, when he's forced to run the newspaper office by himself, he gives away the store, selling classifieds and thank you notes at 25-year-ago prices.

That's why, at the end of the day when the office grows quiet and he's alone, the editor walks to the front and locks the door from the inside. Then he turns out the light in the outer office and hunkers at his desk, browsing the daily papers from Coffeyville and Topeka. A newspaperman loves to read another paper. It's like a sip of wine to an alcoholic.

Then the phone starts ringing. After frowning during at least five rings, he picks it up and answers, "Chronicle office."

He hopes it is his wife, telling him supper is ready, or maybe a friend reminding him of a city meeting that evening. But there's a good chance that he will scribble down a classified ad for someone wanting to sell their boat. And, rather than handle the detail work, he will leave the note on the front counter, if indeed, he remembers to tear it off his note pad. Chances are better it will go with him to the city council meeting that night.

Then a customer will be unhappy when his boat doesn't

get advertised, and he will get a free ad plus an apology when he calls the editor's wife after the paper comes out.

And the editor will get a good chewing.

Everybody -- the family and the town -- thinks he is absent minded.

In reality, he just needs to let the darn telephone ring.

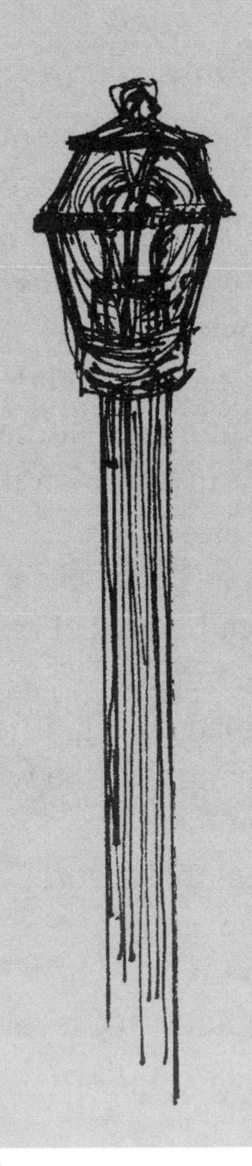

"Off the Cuff"

Words to quash a spat: "You're so right, darling"

Somewhere in the stacks of old phonograph records in our attic is a thick and brittle platter that brings back wonderful memories when I stumble across it.

It was in 1951 that my mother, who loved to dabble in poetry, sent one of her poems to a mail-order recording company in Hollywood. I have no idea how much money the company made her send with her hand-scribbled poem, but it was probably enough to buy a pair of shoes for herself, or maybe even a new dress.

But this was a personal dream of my mother, and I well remember watching her put the envelope in the rural mailbox in front of our farm and wish it well toward its destiny in Hollywood.

It was only a few weeks later that a flat envelope arrived in that same box, and words "Fragile - Phonograph Record," were imprinted on the outside.

Mom had made it big, I figured. Somebody in Hollywood had recorded a song that she wrote. We'd now be rich.

Or so I thought.

Funny thing, that record. We had no way to play it. Fact is, we had only recently gotten electricity at our house, and we certainly had no luxuries such as a record player. We asked a neighbor lady, Kathleen Cleveland, to bring her phonograph player to our house for the debut auditioning of Mom's song,

"You're So Right."

It was never played outside our living room, so obviously, nobody got rich with it.

Today the song is barely audible, what with the many varieties of phonograph needles dragged through its grooves over the years. But through it all, the words of the first verse can be heard, performed by some unknown singer. He probably made fifty such records that day, and immediately forgot the lyrics soon after he sang them:

I met a girl the other day who had the sweetest smile.

I'll bet if you would measure, that smile would reach a mile.

But all the time I watched her, she made me think of you,

And now I'm broken hearted, and staying oh so blue.

You're so right, darling. And I can see it now.

You're so right. Oh, so right.

It has been over a decade since my mother passed from this world, but I shall always recall those three precious words, "You're So Right," vowing to myself to say them more often.

So much has been written about saying, "I'm sorry," and "I was wrong." They definitely have resolved millions of personal conflicts.

But Mom's little song rang out a more positive message -- *you're so right.* And without knowing what little conflict might have inspired her to write it, the song is indelibly etched in my mind

I plan to teach its simple lyrics and melody to my grandchildren in the same spirit that they were taught to me. That way, the little song will live on.

She surely was ... so right.

"Off the Cuff"

Sweet ketchup and homemade bread

Springtime 1953 brought big changes in my life. That was the year Ike took office, Ford stopped making flathead V8 engines, and Timber Hill School dropped sweet ketchup, seasoned green beans and home-churned butter from its daily menu.

The first two were important enough, but the latter item threw a curve in my personal life.

Here's the scoop on the sweet ketchup caper:

Electricity was the only modern utility in our little country school. There was no telephone, no running water, and no indoor restrooms. But, to the kids at Timber Hill, that was pretty normal. Nobody complained about such arrangements. Fact is, it was quite a treat for a first grade boy to raise his hand, always indicating one finger or two, and the teacher would grant him a trek to the outhouse that was located way out at the edge of the school property, near the woods.

It was like an outing -- no pun intended. When the weather was good, a kid could run lickety-split to the little house, take care of business and still have five minutes to sit under a tree and daydream, or watch a squirrel play, or shoot some marbles on the sunny, sandy ground.

But the highlight of each day was lunchtime, because we knew that Mary Epperson, our cook, would place before us a feast fit for a harvest crew. Mrs. Epperson would place the homemade meal on a wooden table in the tiny kitchen, and the children would file by and fill their plates. She would treat us to home-canned vegetables and straight-from-the-farm meats. Homemade rolls were daily fare, and even home-churned butter graced the Timber Hill table.

Then came the real treat -- Mary Epperson's homemade ketchup. It was sweet and thick, almost like jam. We considered it to be dessert, not a topping for fried potatoes.

It was wonderful.

Then at 2:30 each afternoon, the school bell would ring and everybody would head out to recess. And, if there were rolls left over from lunch, Mrs. Epperson would cut them in half, lay a coating of butter on each half, and spread a generous portion of sweet ketchup on top. It was an afternoon treat which would be remembered, at least by this overweight editor, for a lifetime.

But that was all pre-1953.

We all watched one spring day as the county superintendent of schools drove up in her 1949 Chevy and walked straight to the kitchen. For some 15 to 20 minutes, she talked in whispered tones with Mrs. Epperson, then she pivoted on her heels, strode back to the car and drove away.

Our teacher told us the terrible news: The State of Oklahoma was cracking down on school kitchens.

We soon would have a pumphouse and running water installed. The kitchen would be off-limits to students. And, Mary Epperson had been instructed to use only store-bought, sanitized, oleo-ized, bottled, preserved, inspected stuff for her kitchen. In short, it was good-bye to homemade meals and hello to the school lunch routine.

No more home-churned butter. No more sweet ketchup. And, certainly, no more recess treats placed on a table outside in the air where the flies might, heaven forbid, land on a piece of bread.

That was my first brush with the regulatory arm of the government. And I didn't like it one bit.

By the next fall we'd switched to plastic plates with proper dividers, soybean meal-filled hamburgers, margarine on our store-bought bread, and a can opener to gain access.

We had been the last lucky ones to enjoy the culinary talents of Mrs. Mary Epperson.

One more thing. They also raised the price of school lunches from 15 cents to 20 cents that year. I believe that was the year I started getting behind a nickel per day and I've yet to get caught up.

His days of growing up in the country and attending a rural school remain the editor's script as he recalls a lifetime of happy memories.

"Off the Cuff"

A snow storm is more fun when nobody's expecting it

I liked the old-fashioned way of watching the weather.

It was called: Get up in the morning, look out the window and see what kind of day awaits you.

I well remember the winter of 1954 when I was a kid. Nobody in our little town had a clue that a snow storm was moving in from the Rockies. I was awakened by the shriek of two older sisters as they clambered to the windows and described the crystal white wonderland that awaited us outside.

We immediately switched on KGGF radio and heard the announcer say that all area schools were closed for the day. We were thrilled to hear that the big ordnance plant located nearby was advising its workers to stay home. That completed my happiness because my dad worked there.

I remember walking with him to town and swapping tales with other snowbound neighbor men who gathered at an old-fashioned garage and gas station.

That afternoon we went rabbit hunting with Dad carrying his 12 gauge shotgun and me carrying a b-b gun. I remember a neighbor, Ted McMillen, pulling a sled with his Farmall tractor and being among the lucky boys who caught a ride through the streets of that small town.

The next day wasn't much better, and as I recall, schools were closed for three consecutive days. It was a doozy of a storm, and the great thing was: We didn't know it was coming.

The fact that I remember it shows how special it was -- at

least to a third grader who loved the snow.

So today I try not to grouse about snowfall. But I do complain about the high tech forecasting. I think that it was more fun when kids woke up and rushed to the window to check for snowflakes. Hearing all about it five days in advance spoils the fun.

For the record, no, I didn't kill any rabbits with that b-b gun.

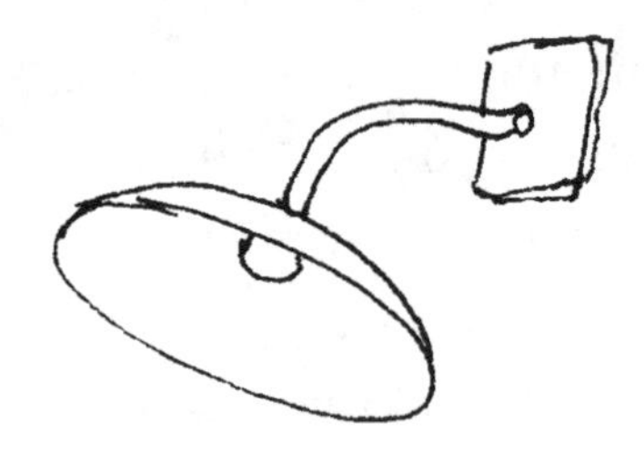

"Off the Cuff"

The saxophone players lost out when the Beatles came to America

It was one of those cultural arts events at our high school and the guy doing the lyceum played a half dozen different wind instruments. There were the tenor sax, clarinet, baritone sax and a couple more.

He played them one at a time and my 1964 classmates were getting a bit restless. Finally, the poor fellow on stage honked out his finale then asked if anyone had questions.

A girl -- I think she was in the sophomore section of the auditorium -- shouted, "What do you think of the Beatles?"

He gave her a puzzled look, shrugged his shoulders and responded, "Who?"

But I can't say I was any better informed. I punched the girl next to me and whispered, "What's a Beatle?"

"It's a singing group from England," she said. "They're scheduled for the Ed Sullivan Show on Sunday night."

OK, I'll admit it. Kansans are always a few months slow in adopting new trends, but this one was too weird to be serious.

What American teenager in his or her right mind would go nuts over a vocal quartet from Liverpool, England?

That shows how smart I was.

I also thought President Kennedy was drugged when he announced that America would put a man on the moon by the end of the decade, and I thought Ford was crazy for dumping its Fairlane hardtop in favor of a new buggy called the Mustang.

Came Sunday night, and my girlfriend (now my wife) and I

rushed home from evening church so we could see the Sullivan Show from its beginning, fearing we might miss this foursome who had turned the entertainment world upside down in the course of two weeks.

It would be the first time any of them had stepped foot on American soil, and certainly the first time most adults had a chance to hear them perform.

I was gulping down my second ham sandwich when Ed Sullivan stepped to the forefront and announced, "Ladies and gentlemen, the Beatles. Let's bring them on." His voice disappeared amid the screams, and the Beatles began.

For a solid ten minutes, there was pure pandemonium in the Sullivan Theatre. Fact is, the four songs performed by the strange looking lads couldn't be heard above the noise of prepubescent girls who tore at their own clothes, jumped up and down and screamed their silly heads off.

They opened with *All My Loving,* then launched into *Till There Was You* – a ballad from the Broadway show *The Music Man*. Next was *She Loves You*, followed by the band's trademark kowtow before the howling audience.

We didn't know it at that moment, but the winds of change blew swiftly that night across our nation, and it has never quite calmed down.

Everyone in my generation remembers where they were when the Fab Four made their debut on the Ed Sullivan Show. It's on the list of where you were when Kennedy was shot, Martin Luther King was assassinated or the night when all television networks broke in to their regular programs to announce that Elvis Presley had died in Memphis.

Actually, the kids in my high school class were quite satisfied with the music before the Beatles changed it all. We liked Bobby Darrin, Fabian, Little Richard, Elvis and Connie Stevens. Remember, it was only six years before the Beatles' arrival that Perry Como's *Find A Ring and You'll Go Round, Round, Round* was No. 1 on the charts for eight consecutive weeks. And Pat Boone's *Love Letters in the Sand* was still ringing in our ears, as was *Oo-ee-oo-ah-ah, Ting-tang-wally-wally-bing-bang*.

The long haired chaps from Liverpool weren't any better than the fellow playing all those saxophones on our stage.

But we all changed, didn't we? Before long, we were singing along with the mop haired Beatles as they sang the songs of love, protest, silliness and soul. Our clothing styles, hair cuts and, yes, even our moral fiber, started to bend when the "singing group from England" hit our shores.

They began a legend, and every popular song composed after Feb. 8, 1964 --- the date of the Sullivan Show -- was influenced by the four names that we never shall forget: John, Paul, George and Ringo.

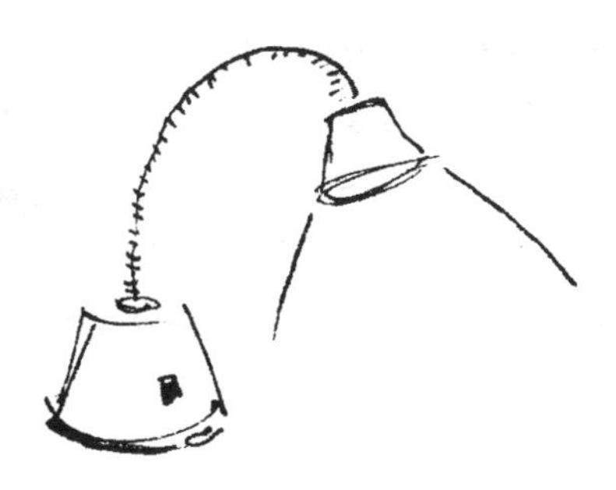

CHAPTER NINE

The other editor

Walking along Main Street and glancing in each store front provides the aging editor two opportunities: First, to nod congenial greetings to the store owner and staff, assuming someone is in there waving back. But equally important to him is the reflection he sees of himself in the big window.

He doesn't like the picture he sees, at least not the human one. The Chronicle editor has battled a chubby middle all his adult life, so what he sees in that mirror-like window reveals it all. He crinkles his brow in frustration.

It is the other image he needs to see, the one of a man who has spent his adult lifetime selling ads on that main street, getting to know each merchant like a family member, reporting news about the town with its up and down times and watching as one business after another closes, thanks to what most people would call progress.

He often has mused that editors don't die of old age. They simply suffocate from trying to live up to readers' expectations. Local people assume the hometown Chronicle will always be there, regardless of how few businesses remain on Main Street.

For that reason, even with his early morning to late night work schedule, the editor has always dabbled in some outside involvement: Teaching part-time in a local community college, making radio commercials, and even serving a couple terms as a county commissioner.

It's not the norm for an editor to do such things. Professional journalists would say he jeopardizes his objectivity as a newspaper publisher. Phooey. He does it to keep oxygen in his blood -- and a few extra dollars in his pocket.

Still, as he walks along that street and grumbles about his portly profile, the editor smiles. He lives his dream every day. His feet hit the floor on the run early each morning because he knows his day will be full of surprises. There are few routines in the life of a newspaperman, other than the deadline, that never take a holiday.

When he walks through the front door of his newspaper office, he knows the plan for his day will change. He always jots down his "to do" list and places it on his desk, and he starts checking off items as they are accomplished.

In nearly 40 years of newspaper publishing, he has never made it to the bottom of the list, because penciled in between lines are the fires he has extinguished as his day progressed.

"I'm going to City Hall," he will holler as he exits the office. "Be back in a few minutes."

En route to the city office he stops by the post office where a reader tells him about a barn that burned during the night. He jumps in his car, making sure there is film in his camera, and turns toward the country road that will lead him to the fire scene.

Clicking his camera and asking a couple questions of the volunteer fire chief, he walks toward his car when a store owner asks him to stop by and pick up an ad.

That's priority No. 1 in this business. So he heads to the furniture store and jots notes for a small ad, not the full page he had envisioned as he drove back from the barn.

A local lawyer sees him emerging from the store and hollers, "Got a minute?"

That leads to another hour of going over details of an upcoming bond election and grousing about the Democrats at the courthouse who kept the lawyer from being appointed as district judge.

Back to the newspaper office, the editor leaves his notes at the front counter and sits down at his typewriter where he starts pounding out small stories from the stack of notes that have accumulated while he was gone.

Folks think editors write editorials from sun-up until dark. They don't. They mostly run from place to place then play catch-up when they get back to the office.

By day's end, he looks at the "to do" list and shakes his head.

"I've got to get organized," he says to himself.

One would think that such a fascinating routine would keep him challenged. Hardly.

The grass on the other side looks lush and green to an out-of-breath editor, so over the years, he has snuck out the back door and quietly imitated someone else for a few hours.

But he always comes back.

Before he opens the front door of his office, he takes that slow stroll along Main Street and waves to the lifeless store windows.

The reflected image of a happy editor is what he needs to see, because it snaps a picture of the life he chose so many years ago. Even if he feels suffocated at times, he knows the town needs the hometown Chronicle, therefore needs him.

He returns to his office and looks at yet another framed saying on his wall. It was penned a century ago by another Kansas editor, William Allen White: *A town without a newspaper just isn't much of a town*.

So, the light on Main Street will glow again tonight.

"Off the Cuff"

The stones may not speak to you but listen for voices in the wind

I always notice cemeteries as I drive from town to town, and there are plenty of them to see.

Sometimes I pull into a shady cemetery just to see the beauty, often taking a stroll to look at names and dates on tombstones. I've stopped in a cemetery many times to eat a convenience store sandwich. I know that sounds strange, but it's so quiet there and keeps me from eating while driving down the highway.

There's a cemetery located three blocks from our home, and I often walk there for my daily exercise. Twice around the cemetery is one mile -- two miles if I go up and down every little road.

There simply are times when an ol' newspaperman wants to get away from everything and everybody, and the cemetery offers such solace. Sometimes it's fun to walk on the city streets, waving at neighbors and chatting with friends who pull their cars over to start a conversation. But when a guy wants to be alone, the cemetery is the place to go.

Actually, I'm not alone, am I?

In the local cemetery, there are some 6,500 graves, which far exceeds the population of our town. I have attended dozens of burial services there, and so many of my hometown friends are buried there. Of course, I am also familiar with the names of those whose obituaries were printed in this newspaper.

So, as I take my walk, I often speak to the folks whose names I see on the stones.

"Good morning, General," I say as I walk by the tomb of Gen. George H. Wark.

"Hello, Mr. Bell."

"Hi, Doyle."

"Good day, Mrs. Cain."

I hope I'm not disrespectful. I just like smiling at the memories I find as I view the field of names that have made my life fuller -- even some whose lives ended long before mine started, such as town pioneers.

Sometimes I can't keep myself from stooping over and sweeping the grass clippings from a name plate, or snipping off the wilting peonies from a bush that has bloomed longer than I have been alive.

I marvel at how long many friends have been deceased. Could it really be that long since I saw you?

I always pause at the graves of Kathy's parents. I couldn't possibly walk by without glancing their way and recalling the love and encouragement they gave us, the direction they provided, and the legacy they left to build upon.

Funny thing: I can't make myself run or jog through a cemetery. Wouldn't be proper.

There is one tombstone with a built-in granite bench -- the perfect place for a little breather. From there I look a distance and see the town, hear its sounds and feel its activity. People are dashing here and there, trying to get their day's work done and planning a tomorrow that, in most cases, they never once doubt will be there.

Then I see the names of many whose tomorrow never came, at least on this side of the big river, and I realize how unsure life can be and I immediately push my shoulders back and increase my steps, devoting my day to a renewed appreciation of my family and friends who are still walking and talking, and committing myself to being a better listener, observer and friend.

So, as you prepare for Memorial Day, I'm sure you will find yourself driving through a cemetery where loved ones are at rest. I can only encourage you to take some time to walk among the stones, smile at the memories, and perhaps speak the name of those who made your life fuller and richer.

They may not speak back to you.

But listen to the wind, and hear them anyway.

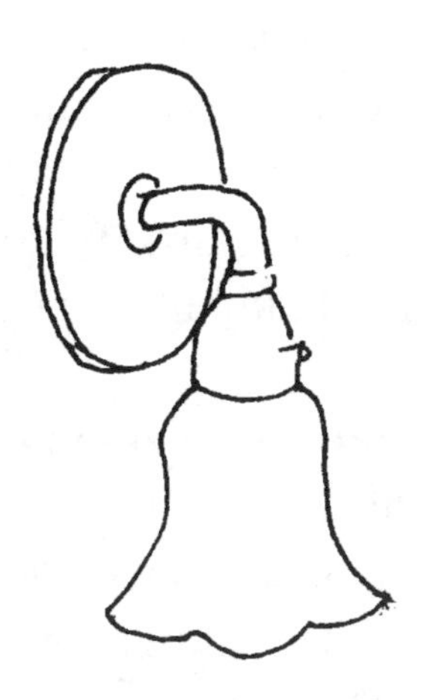

"Off the Cuff"

Yes, the pigs sounded pitiful but their eyeballs were great toys

The declining condition of today's hog market has caused pork prices to plummet, and many Americans are gaining a new appreciation for "the other white meat."

All of a sudden, it's cheaper to buy a pork loin than beef roast, and the swine industry is liking the rave reviews which consumers are giving this always-second-in-line table meat.

When I was a kid we always ate pork, both because it was cheap, and it was easier to keep in our less-than-efficient refrigeration system. We made good use of a smokehouse for hams, bacon, sausage and other cured cuts, and we seldom ate pork roasts and other fancy cuts.

Beef, on the other hand, required proper freezers so we sold most of our calves rather than butchering them and kept the pigs for Sunday meals.

I also remember seeing hams hanging along the underside of our neighbor's dug well (the big, wide ones -- not the pipes in the ground). I can remember the wonderful aroma of that well when I would stick my head into the opening and peer downward where the reflection of my face created an eerie sight. I also remember the echoing sound which my voice would make as I hollered down into the century-old well.

In today's world, I'm sure such damp old wells would be condemned by the health department, and nobody in their right mind would consider hanging hams down inside such a musty cavern.

Still, thoughts of those primitive methods are overshadowed by memories of the wonderful meals which came from the smokehouse, and the side dishes which my mother and both grandmothers would prepare.

We ate sausage burgers, rather than hamburgers. We enjoyed plenty of pork tenderloin, ham, ribs, bacon -- the usual cuts. But we also ate brains and eggs, and my grandma loved tongue sandwiches. Our family had a specialty called hogity-paw which was cornmeal mush with added shreds of lean pork shaven from the inside of the ol' hog's head.

My mother always made hogity-paw sound like the best thing this side of Heaven. When combined with scrambled eggs and Grandma's homemade biscuits, it certainly lived up to its billing. But more than anything, it was cheap. And that brings us back to today.

Hogs are good eating -- but sometimes not good in the money-making department.

I recall so many "slaughter days" when neighbors would congregate to butcher a whole passel of hogs. It was quite a sight for a young boy to witness, and I shall never forget the greasy doorknob on our kitchen door on the day when the neighbors would come over and slaughter.

I remember the squealing pigs as they found themselves in a no-win trap; the snap of a .22 rifle; the men joking with each other as they hoisted each hog up high and started their nauseating job of ripping open the undersides and letting everything splat into waiting tubs.

I recall the women helping to cut and package the meat and the men preparing the hickory fire in the smoke house. And I remember the stern warnings for all the kids "not to open that door" for several days.

So, cheap pork has its advantages -- like rekindling memories of days gone by when hogity-paw was our caviar, buckets full of lard were sent home with every visitor and playing with pigs' eyeballs was the greatest fun a kid could experience.

Chicken, turkey and emu ranchers could never relate to that one.

"Off the Cuff"

We inaugurated more than Ike

We were an excited bunch of kids the day President Eisenhower was inaugurated 53 years ago this week.

Don't get me wrong. I, and fellow first graders in the country school near Bluejacket, Okla., didn't know much about Ike and his famed heroism from W.W.II. We were unfamiliar with the young senator who was his running mate, Richard Nixon. We knew of no issues separating Ike from the outgoing president.

Those were people and events for the "big people" to worry about. We had a more important event on our minds.

We were about to see our first television set.

Every grade in the Timber Hill school included a member of the Epperson family, and it was their parents who invited all 49 students from our school to come over and watch the inaugural parade.

Since Christmas we had enviously admired their big TV antenna ... the first on the hill. Their house, which was home to a dozen kids, was an unlikely site for Timber Hill's first boob-tube. It was not a shanty, mind you, but neither was it a castle.

Still, it had one thing none of our homes contained -- a 13-inch, round-screen Crosley television set. KVOO-TV in Tulsa was the talk of the Epperson kids when they came to school each morning.

They talked about Howdy Doody, Milton Berle and Arthur Godfrey. They watched *Lassie* and Ed Sullivan on Sunday nights and *The Lone Ranger*, *Fury* and *My Friend Flicka* on Saturday mornings.

Suddenly, the Eppersons were the best informed folks at Timber Hill as they dropped such names as Douglas Edwards and Edward R. Murrow. The rest of us still tuned across the radio band to pick up Glenn Condon on KRMG in Tulsa. And while the radio version of *The Roy Rogers Show* was pretty good, we longed to see the King of the Cowboys ride down his happy trail into the televised sunset.

But this day our thoughts were turned to politics and to the kind invitation extended us by the Eppersons. We went two grades at a time and walked down the sandy road to their house where our teacher threatened us with bodily torture if we even touched the new fangled gadget.

We watched in awe as the tiny set flickered and squawked, each of us daydreaming of the time when all would have our own TV set to watch, and one of those handsome antennas crowning the ridge of each roof.

Time moved swiftly for TV and for the kids at the Timber Hill School. The schoolhouse is now used as a hay barn and the Eppersons moved away to California long ago.

We suspect that they, wherever they are today, watched this year's version of the presidential inaugural either live or on replays of the evening news.

We wonder if they might recall the day when they gave 49 country kids the thrill of our lives ... with a flick of the switch on their 13-inch Crosley.

CHAPTER TEN

Writing his weekly column

He likes to encourage others, but intentional efforts by the Chronicle editor to do so usually fall flat.

The same goes for writing intelligent, thought-provoking columns. He will spend hours writing a piece that he thinks is sure to win the Pulitzer Prize.

Nobody will say a word about it.

Then, under deadline, he will pen a simple, from-the-heart poignant tribute to a 90-year-old former school janitor, and his readers want to lift him to their shoulders in celebration.

Or he will write something about his days of attending a one-room school in the hills of Oklahoma, and everyone applauds.

It's a real maze, this thing of writing. A small-town editor starts each day pondering events, issues and personalities and see-saws his way through each letter and every word he writes. Readers like his homespun humor and recall of the old days, and he relishes thoughts of the 1950s when everything seemed simpler, easier and somehow nicer.

Still, he grimaces when the old coots two generations his senior dote on the "good ol' days" and never do a thing to bring about a good tomorrow. So he darts back and forth with his writing, sometimes penning editorials about the state legislature or the local school board, but invariably scooting them aside as he sits down to write his column,

"Off the Cuff."

In nearly 40 years of publishing the Chronicle, he has never missed an edition with that column. Over those years, his columns have been quoted on the floor of the U.S. Congress, read by Paul Harvey and National Public Radio and picked up by newspapers and magazine, large and small. Still, he grimaces when he thinks about those particular columns, calling them lightweight and emotional.

His best writing goes unnoticed. Or so he thinks.

He writes about little episodes of everyday life in a small Kansas town. Even when it's about something in his own life, he tries to write in such a way that readers will identify, see themselves between the letters and lines, and somehow respond.

His wife often has told him, "If you could make money by making old girls cry, we'd be rich."

She was right, of course.

When a bumbling editor writes sweetness about a child, or an old man in the nursing home, or a favorite teacher from 50 years ago, the emotions pour out.

When he writes about something in the national news and gives it a humorous spin, local folks stop him on the street to say they really liked his "story" this week.

And, when he hurts inside, those feelings often are relayed through "Off the Cuff," but never on purpose. Those are the ones that get quoted in other newspapers and on the radio. He has never figured out exactly why, but he secretly cherishes the compliments, vowing to write a column next week that will really wow 'em. And that's when he fails, because he invariably will write about some boring issue such as the need for a taxpayers' bill of rights.

Then he makes a complete circle and accidentally writes something thoughtful, uplifting, funny, tearful, pithy, or perhaps zany.

He sits in his office each evening, pondering this jig-saw, wondering why people continue to read the Chronicle and how his columns fit into the puzzle.

That's when the telephone rings and a reader screams at him for spelling their daughter's name Casey instead of Kasee, or the mayor stops his subscription because his recommendation to rename Main Street to "Korean and/or Vietnam Motorcyle Veterans Memorial Avenue for Freedom" didn't merit an editorial endorsement. Then he smiles to see a local sixth grader drop two quarters in the news rack outside the office and broadly smile at the picture on the front page -- a group shot of her softball team.

They're all lights to the hometown editor. Their responses to the Chronicle will cause him to start tomorrow afresh, looking around the town so he can pen a "story" that will keep local folks among his readers for another week.

"Off the Cuff"

Writing to Cousin Doyle on a little chunk of rock

A little flat rock, maybe eight inches in diameter, is my litmus test for today's postal carriers.

On the quiet country road where I grew up, it was with great anticipation that the rural mail carrier arrived each day. Jimmy Talley was his name and service was his game.

I'm not just talking about stuffing letters and catalogs in our mail box. He also was our communication with the outside world.

The last of five children, I spent my preschool years at home with my mother, and it sometimes got pretty quiet around the old home place. While my mom tried -- with plenty of success -- to make each day fun for me, I was fully aware that the nearby country school was teeming with energy. In my mind, I just knew that every other boy in Oklahoma was spending his day riding the merry-go-round, playing baseball and shooting marbles. Meanwhile I was helping my mom do the dishes.

So, when Jimmy Talley's car topped the hill just west of our place, it was a big deal to me.

I never received letters or packages. My mail was more personalized. As Jimmy pulled to a stop in front of our house, it wasn't unusual to see him reach under his front seat and pull out a block of wood or a flat rock with a message scrawled in chalk on its face.

"That's for Rudy," he would tell my mother. "His cousin Doyle sent it to him."

And I usually had a matchbox full of secret stuff for Jimmy to deliver two miles to Doyle's house on the next day's route.

I also remember Jimmy Talley stopping to douse a trash fire in our back yard one morning. And when the neighbor's bull broke down the gate and found his way to our pasture, my mother knew where to find help. She left a note in the mailbox for Jimmy Talley, and by mid-morning the amorous Hereford was back in his own bedroom, thanks to a 15-minute detour by a helpful mail carrier.

Of course, I don't expect today's USPS carriers to do such things, although I'm sure they would perform such neighborly gestures if their rules allowed it.

Still, it galls me a little to receive a note from a reader in Topeka with this message: "We enjoy the Chronicle so much, but it sometimes takes five full days for it to get here."

Sure, I realize our hillbilly community back in the 1940s and 1950s was idyllic and that my memories probably are more melancholy than real, but ... a rock from my cousin Doyle? And without a zip code?

Unfortunately, Jimmy Talley died a few years ago, taking with him some wonderful secrets to postal delivery.

We don't want to return to the days of delivering rocks to country cousins, but we often wonder if today's automated, bar coded, zipped and zoned mail wouldn't get there faster if the top managers had a few Jimmy Talleys in their midst.

"Off the Cuff"

We didn't need electricity to bring us into the light

Electricity made its debut in the Taylor home 50 years ago this summer.

Before then, our house was lighted by coal oil lamps and our upright RCA radio operated by use of two dry cell batteries. My mother mashed potatoes the old fashioned way and hemmed a pair of pants using a treadle sewing machine.

We dreamed of the day when our house would be wired and each room would have its own light bulb hanging from the ceiling. And in the summer of 1951, our dreams came true.

Our house had been built seven years earlier, a year before I was born, but my parents couldn't afford the modern conveniences of electricity, telephone or running water. It was to be a rock house, but it was several years before they could hire a stone mason to lay up the exterior. But inside that house with the dimly lit rooms, and the black paper covering the outside, and the pot-bellied stove gracing the living room, we found something that electric power could never generate: Happiness.

It wasn't the dark ages. In fact, most of our neighbors had electricity. But that delay in joining the modern world may have been the best move my parents ever made. It made for long evenings, lots of singing, playing simple games and going visiting.

I don't think a week ever went by that we didn't go visit a neighbor for an entire evening. More importantly, the neighbors came to the Taylor home.

My dad was a self-taught barber, giving free haircuts to all the boy-type cousins on Sunday afternoons. And, until '51, the shears were hand-clippers. They didn't make a buzzing sound and they really didn't do too good a job at cutting hair. They sort of hacked it off in neat little clumps. But a smooth job with the scissors and comb gave the desired result.

When one stops to think about all the modern conveniences we enjoy today, it seems impossible that we could ever have lived without them. We take them so for granted.

Believe me, I wouldn't want to do without today's wonderful air-conditioning, clothes washer and dryer, television, computer, lights of all kinds, and all the kitchen appliances which help keep us chubby and contented. But as I recall, we once lived a life that was just as happy, and there was no shortage of chubby Taylors in our living room.

Most of all I remember getting up early that special morning in the summer of '51 and waiting to see the men arrive who would wire our house and turn on the lights.

Now I know the truth.

A brighter place never existed than that little country home.

And that was before we flipped on the power.

"Off the Cuff"

Sometimes the Grit method looks mighty tempting

Lots of readers give me clips from other newspapers, and this week I noticed one of them from *Grit Magazine*.

I haven't seen a *Grit* in many years, but I understand it now is published in Topeka rather than Williamsport, Pa., where I sent the weekly proceeds of my first newspaper route at the age of 12.

I always liked the name *Grit*. While I can't remember whether the Sun-Times is in Chicago or St. Louis, or whether there is a hyphen between Capital and Journal at Topeka, I have no trouble at all remembering *Grit*.

There has been only one *Grit*, even though it has evolved from the raggedy tabloid that I sold door to door to the slick magazine that it is today.

It was my first job, and my mother helped me fill out the order form and mail it to Williamsport. Two weeks later I was officially accepted as a "Grit Boy." I watched for that letter to arrive every day, and finally I watched with glee as the rural mail carrier poked a big brown envelope in our box.

Inside, I found a newspaper bag made of white canvas. It had four letters printed in bold red ink on the front: G-R-I-T.

How proud it made me to stuff my order of 15 newspapers inside that bag. I must have stood in front of the mirror for a solid half hour to admire my new look.

It was a look that never changed, because from that moment

until today, I've always had some connection with newspapers.

I wrote news articles for my Future Farmers of America chapter when I was in high school.

I also was an official assistant to the pretty daughter of the Chronicle publisher and we ran a twice-a-week newspaper route during the three years that we dated in high school.

I'm not sure if it was the aroma of printer's ink or her *Hypnotic* perfume that snagged me, but I'm still her official assistant today.

I've engaged in all kinds of publishing ventures over the years to include magazines, sports tabloids, newspapers and newsletters.

So I'd say *Grit* magazine had quite an impact on that 12-year-old kid back in the 1950s.

* * *

I can still remember the exact route. Nobody actually subscribed to *Grit* in those days. They simply handed over 15 cents to their Grit Boy each Saturday morning.

I sold every copy every week and made a total profit of 75 cents -- plenty of money to cover my expenses for the coming week.

My mother would help me count the money, fill out the form and make out her personal check for the other two-thirds which belong to the company.

Every time I get discouraged with today's expensive business methods, or frustrated about everything from taxes to insurance to personnel matters, I find myself pondering whether it might just work if I simply printed a newspaper edition then went out each Saturday morning and peddled copies door to door.

I could cancel the 15 telephone lines that our newspaper has in our four offices, along with our seven e-mail addresses, tax numbers that get so confusing, and a payables file that gets mighty fat before the end of each month.

When the roof leaks and mailing expenses grow like the national debt, enabling our newspaper to be delivered via the U.S. Mail the day after printing, it sure makes me rethink the *Grit* method of doing business:

Just make newspapers. Walk door to door. Quit when tired. And keep the money in a cigar box.

It's something for an over-the-hill publisher to think about as today's edition comes rolling off the press.

For the record, I really do give a lot of credit to that perfume for piquing my interest in newspaper publishing.

For all its notoriety, printer's ink still smells like a dirty diaper.

It's the tales that go with the ink that makes this former *Grit* boy look forward to each new day.

I get up early so I can try to make the percentage of profit that I earned with my *Grit* route.

Cut me in for a third any ol' day.

That sneezy monkey would like "Let's-be-a-friend Day" at church

A popular cell phone company runs funny commercials about phrases thought to be heard when the phone pops, chirps and garbles the words of the caller.

"Get me something old," was thought to be "monkey with a cold" on the receiving end.

The man thought his wife told him to "flour the kids," so the camera showed his children with white powder sprinkled over their heads. The wife actually had said, "How are the kids?"

The commercials are funny, not because they're great humor, but because everyone identifies with such guffaws.

Last Sunday at church, our preacher made the announcement, "Don't forget our lesbian friend day."

I frowned and looked at my wife. "It's *let's-be-a-friend-day*," she whispered.

When I told an employee to drop off the newspaper paste-ups at our house, she brought pay stubs instead.

A reader once called to place this classified ad: "Wanted - pasture for ten thousand calves." Actually, he said, "ten cows and calves." But he liked it because I made him sound so big and rich.

A local waitress handed me the menu and said, "Our nipples are up high."

Actually, she was trying to get me to try their noodles or pie.

I asked an employee to bring me the "bank ad," and she

brought me a band-aid.

Shortly after we got married, I wrote a check at Sears and the clerk asked for our address. "We live at 119 East Hurd," I responded.

The clerk gave me a funny look then quietly replied, "You gotta be kidding — there's really a street named Turd?"

A Baptist mama recalls her childhood when she thought the hymn, "He Arose," started with the words, "Low in the gravy lay Jesus my savior."

Of course, the real words were, "low in the grave He lay ..."

There was a day 35 years ago when I was thrilled to see our family puppy, Candy, lying dead in our driveway.

Let me explain. My wife had called three minutes earlier and screamed, "I just ran over Candy!"

Problem was, I thought she said "Andy," so I went running out the front door of our newspaper office, jumped in the car and zoomed the eight blocks home at 70 m.p.h. There I saw our little son Andy and my wife standing in the driveway looking at the dead dog.

I gave that boy a hug he would never forget, and smiled as I looked at poor little Candy. To the family, it was a tragic day. To me, it was a day of thankful celebration.

So, the TV commercials about the noisy cell phones bring home lots of memories. The older I get, the worse my hearing gets, and the funnier the miscues become.

It makes life more bearable, and a bunch more joyful, if you smile at the storm rather than trying to hide from it.

You might as well enjoy the ride, because a monkey with a cold will only make you sneeze.

Did you say it was your only naked niece?

"Off the Cuff"

Whoever said this was "adult" talk?

The producers of my favorite television show warned last week that viewers should expect to hear unprecedented profanity in next season's scripts.

The show's executive producer said it this way: "Viewers should expect adult language when they watch adult programs."

I'm sorry he missed *Ross Taylor 101* -- the course my dad taught on how to talk. Oh, it wasn't a real class. In fact, my father dropped out of the school following the eighth grade. But he did manage to instill in my heart a wise saying: "A smart person doesn't need to cuss. That only shows how dumb you are."

Famed radio commentator Paul Harvey has already expressed his outrage to on-air profanity. "Yes, I said those words when I was young, but fortunately, I grew out of them," he said. "I don't think profanity is adult talk -- it's junior high trash talk."

So what's the big deal with all this talk about adult themes, adult language and adult scenes?

Beats me. But I fully agree with Dad's philosophy. I have never met a person I thought was smart who uses profanity. It shows shallow thinking. It reveals a limited vocabulary. And it exposes a mind that lacks fulfillment.

Network censors will approve this season's serving of smut, calling it freedom of expression, but it is becoming increasingly apparent that vulgarity on television is getting the upper hand.

Lines are trashy. Themes are silly. Laugh tracks are insidious.

While the debate continues over whether television is mirrored in society in such subjects as sexual abuse, violence and human degradation, it has become painfully obvious that many programs are immersed in such bilge.

There are many refreshing exceptions to the filthy television trend. It would be unfair to paint the entire industry with the brush of smut. But it is disenchanting to see such a centerpiece of our society slipping so rapidly and so unnecessarily.

Perhaps if the networks heard from their viewers it would make an impact. But more than anything, when we see our favorite shows turning to smut, we could nail the coffin shut if all of us would simply turn off the stupid machine -- the one-eyed monster that swells in each of our living rooms.

There are times when it truly is a boob tube.

CHAPTER ELEVEN

Uplifting friends and seeing their lights

Hometown folks have such a gentle way with the local editor, even though they take pokes at him, tease him when he misspells a name in the news columns, and challenge him on political editorials.

For a man who never gives advice to anyone, he is sought for counsel anytime a friend --- even a distant one -- drops by and sits in his guest chair.

Maybe it's because he is a good listener, a point that his wife will argue. Perhaps it is because the hometown editor is street smart, admittedly a bit tainted around the edges, making people think he might know the answers to life's questions. And maybe it's because, as a young man, he fancied visions of becoming a minister. Whatever the misconception about this man who writes simple stories about hometown events, they like to tell it all to him.

But that's OK.

Confused as he may be about their reasons for wanting to talk with him, he always obliges. That's because his life has been a series of "lifts" from others, and sometimes he can pass them along to others.

An elderly, hometown neighbor takes the time to write uplifting notes to the Chronicle editor a couple times each year. They're personal, not for publication. The pen and ink calligraphy always concludes with the words, "stay encouraged."

A friend who moved to Vermont, well into her eighties, spent the last 25 years of her retirement sending notes of encouragement to the Chronicle editor and his family.

An artist sends little sketches intended to cheer up the Chronicle staff, hoping they will offset the hurled stones so oft received.

For many years, a woman named Little Edna called the Chronicle office each March to say, "Those little dandelions are poking their cute little heads up. Have you seen them?"

The list of encouragers is endless.

Maybe that's why the hometown editor gets the honor of hosting people of all ages, all lifestyles, all political and religious persuasions.

They come, sit and tell their stories.

They don't know it, but they all carry invisible lanterns, apparently unaware that an illuminated editor just might pass along their light beams in the next edition of the hometown Chronicle.

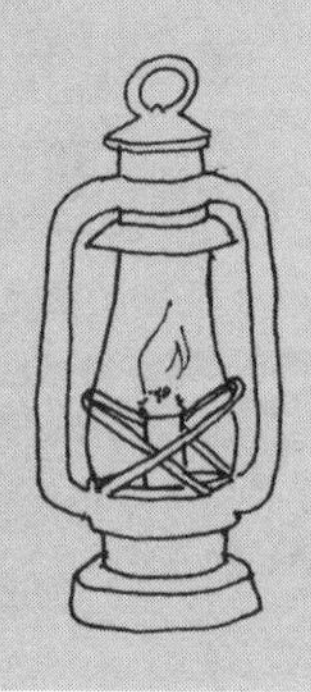

The "Oh, well" society

The nemesis of progress in America has boiled down to two little words:

Oh, well.

When a store clerk totally screws up an order and a miffed customer goes storming out the door, there predictably comes the response from the clerk.

Oh, well.

A family rents a movie after checking to make sure it has a PG or PG-13 label. Then after hearing the infamous "f" word uttered 50 times, somebody in the room comments, "I don't know why they put such filthy language in movies these days."

Then comes the clincher.

Oh, well.

Last night, a group of teenagers sat outside our office while we worked on the Chronicle deadline. One of them sat his droopy rear-end atop one of our flower boxes, smashing several of the flowers. When we told him that he was ruining our flowers, he slowly walked away, shrugged and mumbled, "Oh, well."

Parents are saying it when they lose control of their kids. Students say it after flunking an important test. Neighbors say it when their city leaders shrug off the enforcement of ordinances and the showing of pride. Employees say it to their bosses. And bosses say it to their customers.

Church members say it to their preacher. Husbands say it to

their wives. Heck, if we only knew, dogs probably repeat this popular line to cats.

It's the perfect excuse, and a genuine cop-out.

Uttering those two words solves no problems; pays no bills; excuses no blunder; builds no pride; calms no fears; and clears no air.

"Oh, well" simply says: "Ho hum, let someone else worry about this one."

Problem is, that someone probably is queuing up to express the same sentiment to "someone" else.

And the game goes on.

It makes us wonder, what if these great men and women in history had said "Oh, well" rather than taking the actions they took:

Paul Revere: "The British are coming.... (oh, well)."

Abraham Lincoln: "All men were born to be free ... (oh, well)."

Ronald Reagan: "Mr. Gorbachev, tear this wall down ... (oh well.)"

Mother Teresa: "When my children cry out, I must go to them ... but, oh well."

Winston Churchill: "We will meet our enemy in the streets. We will meet them in the trenches. We will meet them in the air, on the seas ...(yawn) oh, well."

The Book of Genesis: "And God created the heavens and the earth, and all the fish of the sea and all the animals that walk, then He created man and woman, and He said ....oh, well."

Get the picture?

None of us knows when our words will echo into history, whether in the pages of books, or simply repeated by our children as they continue walking in our steps.

Will they be “oh, well” citizens of this world?

We surely hope not, because those two words are paralyzing an already lethargic society, making us sound like the wimps which we apparently enjoy being.

We once were so joyful, hopeful and even eloquently bold in our search for happiness, and pursuing the building of a great nation.

But .... oh, well.

"Off the Cuff"

The TV picture is usually clear unless the pipe to Tulsa is plugged

My mother, who raised five children, always had a simplified quip to explain complex issues.

I remember asking how babies were made.

"Your mama and daddy have a talk with God and that's it," she said.

A half century later, I can't think of a better response, just in case somebody ever asks me that question.

As a second grader, I traded a pocketful of marbles for a tattered deck of cards. Such trades were the daily ritual of a 15 minute school recess.

When I got home, I proudly showed the cards to my mom and asked, "Could you show me how to play cards?"

She never uttered a word. She opened the wood stove that heated our home, grabbed the cards, tossed them in the fire and slammed the iron door shut.

I got the message, probably a bit clearer than I did the one about creating babies.

But my greatest recollection was asking her how movies got to the theater and up on the screen.

"They come from Hollywood," she said.

"But how do they get from Hollywood to the movie theater," I asked.

"The pictures go along the rivers, under the bridges, down the ditches," she said.

"You mean like a big pipe?"

She hesitated. "Yes, sort of like a big pipe."

So, a couple years later when I saw my first television set, I asked her, "Do those pictures come from Hollywood, too?"

"No," she said. "They come from Tulsa --- under the bridges, along the creeks."

So, with those explanations of technology and creation, you can begin to understand why I am so critical of the movie industry, evolutionists and casinos.

Mama didn't allow any of them in our kitchen.

I often wonder if modern society doesn't get too deeply stressed over day to day issues. We feud over whether it's right or wrong to do genetic research. We turn deaf ears to vulgarity and pornography, ironically being told they're protected by the U.S. Constitution. We show explicit illustrations, albeit stick figures, to kindergartners just to make sure they understand the baby conception process. And our state's lawmakers look at gambling as a sure financial source to pay for our schools.

Mama said no.

Talk to God. Don't waste your time gambling. And, let somebody else worry about how the movies get from Hollywood to that big screen.

From there, you can get into more serious matters like learning to read books, play ball, draw pictures, do chores, appreciate music, and share your stuff with others.

Then, as an adult, you possess good perspective on morals, habits and basic philosophies of life.

Still, even today at the age of 60, I never drive over a bridge that I don't wonder what's playing at the local theater or on TV. After all, if the creek beds are deep and the big pipe isn't plugged, you can get pretty good reception from Hollywood, Tulsa and all those other worldly places.

But a good game of poker is still off limits.

Darn it.

"Off the Cuff"

You know you're getting old if you remember your first pizza

If you're any older than me -- and that segment of society gets smaller every day -- you probably don't like pizza.

Oh, sure, senior citizens buy the stuff, but they don't thrive on it like younger folks do. Next time you're in a pizza restaurant, just look around at the customers. Chances are, they're almost all under 50. That's because they grew up sinking their teeth in the cheese-filled crust that has become America's favorite food.

If the customer orders his pizza with a cup of coffee, you know he's over 60.

I was 12 years old when my older sister, 16, came home from a date with more than usual excitement. "We had pizza pie!" she exclaimed. "We went to Bohman's Drive-In and ate pizza pie."

My parents and I gave her a strange look.

Karen then described it. "It's mostly cheese, tomato sauce and hamburger meat," she said, "and they serve it in a big round crust."

It sounded hideous. But then, my mom was a great cook so I never did see the thrill of eating at restaurants and drive-ins. What was wrong with roast beef, pork chops or fried chicken?

Well, it didn't take long for my sister to get a recipe and make us a homemade pizza pie. I remember that my mom and dad didn't care much for it, but they were thoughtful enough to brag on Karen's pizza.

But for me, it tasted delightful.

From that moment until today, pizza has been a part of my life. It was a contemporary to my first date and first kiss. Mmmm -- such spice!

In the early 1960s, there were only two or three pizza restaurants within a 50 mile radius of my hometown. Pizzaria owners, fearing that pizza might be a fad, stuck with downtown locations and former gas stations for their red and white checkered tables and big ovens.

By the late '60s, pizza restaurants dotted the larger comunities, but small-town teenagers still had to drive a distance to find our pizza.

Today, every town of any size has a *Pizza Hut*, and you can actually find good pizza in most convenience stores. But the majority of pizzas consumed in this country come from the frozen section of your local supermarket and then baked at home in the oven.

So, if you're under 50, you don't remember a world without pizza. In fact, it's a staple in your diet -- now finding its place on school lunch menus.

There are pizza parties, pizza potato chips, pizza burgers and pizza flavored muti-vitamins.

I don't know what my parents ate when they were teenagers, but I'm sure they had something that delighted the taste buds and created a party atmosphere for everyone at the table.

I'm just glad this tangy food came along in time for one ol' newspaperman who has added a half dozen inches to his waste by consuming too many rounds of crust filled with cheese and tomato sauce.

And if I ever start ordering a cup of decaf coffee with my pizza pie, I hope somebody kicks the chair out from under me.

"Off the Cuff"

Outsourcing might not be an old newspaperman's thing

The editor of *Esquire* magazine wrote quite an article this week, revealing his secret to life, whether business or personal. It is summed up in one word: Outsourcing.

Editor A.J. Jacobs said he outsources almost everything, from ordering his food to fighting with his wife.

If he wants to tell a bedtime story to his children, he turns on a recorded TV tape made by a professional. He hires a consultant to remember his secretary's birthday and send flowers to his wife on their wedding anniversary. He looks to a travel agent to figure out where he and his wife will go on vacation this year.

He asked a telemarketing company in Bangalore, India, to call his elderly parents twice a week, and a local accountant to pay his bills.

He even asked for a raise at *Esquire* by hiring an internet consultant to design a website just for that purpose. His boss sent an e-card telling him to check the site for a surprise, and there he found all the reasons why he should not give Mr. Jacobs a raise. It didn't work, but the editor deserved an E for effort.

So I've been thinking. If that works for the *Esquire* editor, why not the publisher of a small weekly newspaper in Kansas?

I could take complaints about our newspaper by referring them to a telephone number in India. I could hire inmates at the state penitentiary to call my banker and give excuses for being late on my loan.

I could skip church and ask the minister to e-mail his sermons to me. Tithes would be paid by an automatic bank draft and prayers would be uploaded via the worldwide web.

I could argue with my wife via instant messaging and feed the dog using a robotic dispensing system, much like a candy machine. One bark and Fluffy gets water. Two grrrr's and out plops a Gainsburger.

All local merchants will run a full page ad once ad a month or else get hassled every hour on the hour and through the night by my telemarketer in India.

My palm pilot can be programmed to say all the right things to my wife at bedtime, and a strap-on electric shaver will make my face smooth as I drive to work -- hands free.

But even if I do all this outsourcing ...

... when my little granddaughter reaches up for me, I'll still melt.

... when my three grandsons hug my neck all at once, I'll still squeeze them with joy.

... when my wife puts her arms around me, I'll still forget my troubles.

Actually, dear reader, I think the editor of *Esquire* just might have to do this outsourcing alone. A small-town newspaperman probably couldn't get all those technologies to work anyway. I'd probably order pizza by delivery and get dog food instead.

And, knowing me, I would enjoy every bite of it.

CHAPTER TWELVE

We have this moment today

Main Street in any small town looks mighty different today than it did 50 years ago.

Shoppers head to the mall in a nearby city and the big discount stores are staying open 24 hours a day while offering merchandise cheaper than local merchants can buy the stuff.

So downtown merchants in rural America have, by necessity, changed their way of doing business.

When a jewelry store closes, the local hardware store starts carrying a selection of watches, rings and necklaces.

When the hardware store goes out of business, the owner of the drugstore goes to the auction and buys the jewelry counter and merchandise, adding a few trinkets and toys to dress up the display.

And when the drugstore closes, a second-hand store in the old bank adds the whole array of rings and trinkets to their collection of used clothing, antiques and velvet art of Jesus and John Wayne.

The Chronicle editor doesn't stew over such transitions. He knows the town still has value, even if the storefronts are starting to look shabby.

He vows that the hometown Chronicle will figure out new ways to make enough money to print a weekly newspaper. And, he still gets excited when someone drops by the office to say, "We're opening a new business up the street in the old furniture store."

He immediately envisions a department store that will advertise a full page ad every week. But he knows it will be another antique store that seldom will place an ad in the newspaper.

Change is inevitable.

It is good for a town to ponder its future and make changes to keep it moving forward. Some towns die in the process. Others, mostly those located adjacent to big cities, thrive. But mostly, the small towns across America reconsider their purposes every day and try to be the best places on the map they can be.

That's where the editor falls in line -- with the folks who still see good, even when the chips are down. He keeps the words of gospel music writer Bill Gaither in his heart: "Yesterday is gone and tomorrow may never come, but we have this moment today."

Faith pulls everyone through the tough times. Each time he adheres to that rule, his pathway brightens. It happens because people carry light into his world every time they bring in a news item, or buy a small ad, or simply say hello as they drop two quarters into the cigar box on the front counter -- the price of hometown light for another week.

"Up" in little Jenny's world

Little Jenny tapped me on the knee this morning and asked, "Daddy, do you like up or down the best?"

I thought for a minute then threw it back at her. "I don't know, Jenny -- which do you like best?"

"I think I like up," she replied. "I don't like down."

Following that philosophical exchange, I've concluded:

1. The kid is definitely a Republican.
2. She's destined for the stars.
3. She's smarter than most adults who don't know up from down.

But Jenny's innocent question made me think over a few things. Am I usually up, or do I drag myself and others down with my words and actions?

Am I "up" on my hometown and all those I encounter each day? Do people feel better after reading my newspaper, or do I portray a world of gloom to them?

When I think of my future, do I look upward toward the heavens, or southward to the other place?

Granted, Jenny's question may have been typical three-year-old yacking. But for a moment or two, it made this dad sit back and think. I slowed my pace for a while, thought over my priorities in life, and came to one big conclusion:

I'm with little Jenny.

I like "up."

And the world would be a happier place if we all were three years old.

"Off the Cuff"

Dad is not a digital concept, so GOOGLE won't find him

Most internet users fall into one of two categories: Googlers or Yahooers.

I Google.

Several times each day I type in the words G-O-O-G-L-E and search for information: Maps, word definitions, airline tickets, names of government officials -- you name it and Google or Yahoo will find it.

That's why, as I sat down to write a Father's Day column this morning, I first logged onto the Internet and typed: *www:dad.com*. Nothing.

I then typed *www:dad.net*. Zero.

Same with *www:dad.org*. In all cases the computer screen showed the same message: Address not found.

It proved my point. In a day when all of us look for important resources in high-tech places, we still must seek "home" to find a dad.

That discovery was not exactly monumental. Every major religion in the world emphasizes the importance of fatherhood -- and that's the family kind, not just the breeding variety. Old Testament prophets sounded the alarm that tribal fathers needed to be living examples for their children to follow.

Other Bible writers echoed the same sentiments, touting the virtues of teaming-up with Godly mothers and the vital mission of "training up your children as they should go, and when they are old they will not depart from it."

Today, any judge will tell you that such old-fashioned concepts are missing from all-too-many homes. Homes often are not led at all, and unguided children find themselves in all sorts of trouble ... and our society becomes the collective victim.

Personally, I feel quite inadequate as a father, an admission that most dads will make. Still, being a father is a thrill unlike anything I have ever experienced. It is an honor and privilege. And I thank God every day that my two sons and one daughter always treat me with love and respect. It definitely is an honor I do not deserve, yet I bask in it.

Nothing, but nothing, makes my day more than answering the telephone and immediately hearing a voice on the other end that simply says, *"Hi, Dad."*

Pure ecstasy.

That's why I'm glad the computer screen shrugs its shoulders when "Dad" is searched on the Internet ... and he is not there.

"Off the Cuff"

Bootin' out Baby Bill

Baby Bill isn't looking forward to Christmas.

The grubby, tattered, hairless baby doll, age one year and the only possession that really matters to our little daughter Jenny, age 2 1/2, is about to get the boot.

At least, that's the plan. But we haven't discussed it with little Jenny.

Last Christmas, Jenny received two dolls. One was a lovely thing, resembling Farah Fawcett or Bridget somebody. The other doll was a K-Mart cheapo. Why Jenny's mother bought our precious little daughter this bald, wobbly, naked "thing" is anybody's guess.

But when everybody else is down on Jenny, she knows Baby Bill will be there in all his smelly glory. He's been flushed in the stool twice but refused to swirl and sink. He's been thrown in the dishwasher, and once he spent two weeks in the dog house with Fluffy.

Frankly, I don't even like the name "Bill." It reminds me of those statements I receive at month's end. But Jenny won't hear of any other handle.

He's Baby Bill.

And he is a she. I think.

The reason I'm making jokes about Baby Bill is that little Jenny is about to get a new baby doll, a luscious blonde from one of those big stores in Tulsa. It's got a full wardrobe of clothes, coiffable hair, glistening eyes, and a $30 price tag.

My stroke of genius, you see, is to replace Baby Bill. Maybe

I'll stick him in an old trunk in the attic or put the unsightly, broken-up little guy out of sight for good.

But I have a feeling this dad is about to get the ol' double-whammy straight from my little girl's eyes. Although she tells me every night how she would like one of those dolls on page 148 of the Sears catalog, she sure has been clinging to Baby Bill this week.

She feeds him scrambled eggs, paints his toe nails and changes his diaper. She talks to him, prays for him and falls to sleep with Baby Bill tucked under her chin.

When he's lost, we get the whole family out to search the premises. And when he's found, she squeezes him with glee.

So, come Christmas morning, we'll find out who's boss around the Taylor place -- little Jenny and that flea-bitten doll of hers, or Dad and his life-sized, sanitized, beautified, plasticized replacement.

Somehow, I have a feeling Jenny will win out, and Baby Bill will be spared a trip to the attic.

Because down deep, I've come to love him, too.

Someday, I'm going to write a book on how that little girl has turned my world upside down. Until she came along, I had everything figured out.

Now I find myself abandoning international issues to write editorials about baby dolls.

And I even admitted I loved Baby Bill.

Good grief.

"Off the Cuff"

A promise finally honored

I nervously clutched the long-stem rose in my hand as I walked onto the dance floor of my daughter's senior prom. I looked in vain for her in the dark gymnasium which was so full of excitement and young dancers. I stuck out like a grasshopper in a room full of ants.

Actually, I had waited a half hour in the hallway to hear a slow song, not wanting to totally humiliate myself, my daughter and all her friends by trying a fast dance.

"Jenny just left for a few minutes," a friend told me as I strained my eyes to find her. "They're taking senior pictures down in the cafeteria — but she'll be right back."

I sat down in a dark corner, in a metal chair, and waited through two golden-oldie songs from the '60s — my generation. During those songs I made the mistake of reminiscing, thinking of all the wonderful times I've had with that girl.

After raising two boys, my wife and I thought we knew everything about raising kids. But on June 13, 1981, little Jenny changed all that. From the first moment I saw her, I fell in love. And I'll swear on a stack of Bibles that she winked at me the first time I held her.

I wrote lots of columns about her when she was little. She was easy prey — because I watched every move she made, listened to thousands of her stories, bought her a jillion dollars worth of clothes, built a couple dozen playhouses out of cardboard boxes, and made myself learn the words to *Sara Sponda, Ret Set Set*.

And, over the years, I made the promise many times to her, "I'll dance with you at your senior prom."

Never did I dream it would roll around so fast.

I also made lots of failed promises, like: "We'll go fishing a lot." Nope, we went only once or twice, and caught nothing.

I told her I'd teach her to play golf. Oh, sure, we played a few times — but it never did take.

When she was five and still riding a tricycle, I promised to buy her a convertible when she turned 16. I didn't.

But more than anything, I told her so many times that, "I'll come home early tonight." Seldom did I honor that promise, and as I sat in that chair in the dark corner last Saturday night, I regretted standing her up so many times.

Still, I always found redemption in Jenny's eyes because she knew I wanted so much to please her, understand her, make her laugh — or just be her friend. To this day, one look my way, and I know exactly where I stand with my little girl.

The third tune of the slow-song set had just begun, and I was beginning to wonder if I'd made a mistake coming to her senior prom.

Then I looked up to see her standing in the doorway, gazing at me with a beaming smile.

"Oh, you came, just like you promised," she said so sweetly. And from there it was ecstasy for this ol' dad.

I handed her the rose and led her to the center of the dance floor. Gracefully, as though she had found a cake crumb on my face, she swept a tear from my face.

And we danced.

I don't know if dads are supposed to arrive unannounced at proms. And I don't know if I did the dance steps correctly. But this I do know: It was a diamond moment in my life that I shall never forget, because it was a promise made good.

I could have danced all night, no doubt about it. But I left after that one song, handing her back to the young man who brought her to the prom.

I'll relive that moment for the rest of my days, and every time I find myself in one of life's dark corners, I'll surely look toward the doorway to see if a beaming face is looking my way.

And if I see Jenny — even in my mind — I'll dance the dark away.

That's a promise.

CHAPTER THIRTEEN

Staying away from "big stuff"

Because his opinion column is titled, "Off the Cuff," the Chronicle editor sometimes refers to his wife as "Mrs. Cuff."

It is because his journalism training instilled the old third-person rule deep in his heart. Usage of "I" and "me" simply were not allowed when he went to j-school, even in a personal column.

He grew up noticing that style among older editors.

"This writer attended the high school band concert Monday evening," the columns would read.

He tried his best to adhere to that rule and to make his columns sound like writers he knew or read each week.

Then came a day, somewhere in his thirties, when he threw the rule book out the back door. While still clinging to the *Associated Press Style Book* for news writing, he started writing his column and editorials in his own way, giving readers a glimpse of the emotions, beliefs, imperfections and inner struggles that made him human.

It clicked.

There was a time when he wrote columns he knew would be picked up by bigger newspapers in the state. Writing about the obvious, and giving each column a punch-line, drew "pick up" rights with other editors who were too lazy to write their own columns. And when he would throw a punch at politicians or blame the government for some silly antic, he gave those editors an excuse to say the same, but without their names typed neatly below the piece.

His oldest son was still in grade school when he said something that shook the editor. The boy stood on his tip toes to read the paste-up page that contained "Off the Cuff."

"Daddy, is there anything good in this one, or is it all about politics and big stuff?"

From that day on, column writing has been a personal exercise for the Chronicle editor. He always reads it aloud as he writes -- the very reason he pens it early each Sunday morning at home. Maybe it's the old radio man in him, but he finds the columns flow better if they can be vocalized, not just written.

He was totally unaware that the same little son was watching him one morning as he wrote *Off the Cuff*.

As the column was finished, a quiet voice emerged from behind him.

"That was a good one."

To heck with the big-time editors.

Somebody else can write about "politics and big stuff."

There's a town out there that needs to be noticed, admired, bragged on, informed and uplifted. It is local folks who need the light of their hometown newspaper, not the editors in big-city newsrooms who are looking for a "pick up" -- the cheap and easy way to get their column in print for that day.

It was a journalistic lesson taught by a 12-year-old boy, a lesson to which the hometown editor reflects, even today.

"Off the Cuff"

The house that really counts

We read with interest about the U.S. House of Representatives holding hearings on crime and what causes it. We wish them well.

But the U.S. House will get nowhere until "houses" nationwide first are put in order. And they're far from it today.

Without values taught in the home, society will continue to choke on its meager efforts to prevent, control and punish criminals.

Parents have lost control of their kids --young and old alike. But more importantly, too many parents have lost any semblance of direction in their own lives. It's hard to place too much blame on the young thugs who reign in the dark streets. It's their parents who spoiled them. It is their parents who failed to put boundaries on their kids' actions. And, it's parents who dropped any thought of religious training for their children, many claiming it was unnecessary and old fashioned.

Pity the kids who never heard about Moses, Noah, Jonah, Abraham and Jesus. They will grow up to live such empty lives.

So, bully for the lawmakers as they line up in front of the TV cameras to talk tough about crime. We hope their new crime bill will scare the pants off anyone planning to do evil.

But nobody should hold their breath waiting to see the crime rate drop.

That will happen only when people take their marital relationships seriously. It will happen only when kids start seeing sideboards on their impulses. And it will happen only when all of society finally realizes that crime is a result of bad decisions made by every one of us.

Until we all go back and redo those decisions, the United States of America will be plagued by prejudice, ignorance, violence and crime. It will take more than a crime bill to correct our mistakes. It will require a national resurgence in character. When that happens, the assault rifles will gather dust in dark attics everywhere.

"Off the Cuff"

Whatever happened to spit-n-whittlers?

They probably didn't know they were being watched, those old men who sat in stone window ledges or on benches scattered along Main Street, but the bona fide spit-n-whittlers were my childhood heroes.

Whatever happened to them?

Back in the early 1950s they were composed of World War 1 and Spanish American War vets, and they'd spend each afternoon loafing, swapping war tales and, of course, whittling.

I don't recall ever seeing one of them turn out anything recognizable -- just little pieces of wood they'd carry in their pockets. With a sharp knife and plenty of time to hone their skills, they'd talk for a spell, gawk up and down the avenue to see who or what was moving about, and they'd whittle.

They also were the town's best ambassadors. They politely nodded to the ladies, giving them a second glance after they passed by, and they exchanged pleasantries with the merchants and others who traversed their sittin' territory.

My mother, a proper lady, would walk fast by these old gents, pulling me along by the arm. "Don't listen to the words those old coots say," she would warn me. "They're just beer joint bums."

But later, when she'd go into the grocery store to shop, leaving me outside to wait, I'd head toward the spit-and-whittlers where I'd take mental notes of every word spoken.

They probably never said anything important, and my mother might have been disappointed to learn that they seldom used cuss words, especially when they knew a little boy was listening from a distance. It was chit-chat, that's all. But sometimes one of them would tell a tale about his war-time experience, or that of his son who fought in the second world war.

It was euphoria for me.

Today, as I drive through these small towns where we publish weekly newspapers, I see few Main Street loafers. Maybe they stay home and watch *The Bold and Beautiful* or *Oprah* on television -- who knows? But this I do know: These old-time patrols of the sidewalks, city dads emeritus, and unverified-but-still-respected war heroes helped to paint a pleasant picture for one middle aged editor who likes to reminisce more than he really should.

And my idea of growing old with grace, peace and dignity includes plenty of thoughts about playing with grandchildren, helping others, and maybe doing a little writing.

But given a warm, summer day, one just may see me organizing a modern-day version of the downtown spit-n-whittlers.

I've already got a good pocket knife.

Now if I can just learn to spit.

"Off the Cuff"

The little rock actually sang

While visiting Fantastic Caverns near Springfield, Mo., last Sunday afternoon, I stumbled onto something more memorable than the cave turned out to be.

Among the items displayed in the gift shop were several boxes of rocks, all appropriately labeled. But only one caught my eye -- a tiny box with a shiny black rock inside, and a tag that read, "Galena."

In my years of watching technology advance to where it is today, including the computer in front of me as I write, nothing ever compared to the Galena rock which rang out the sounds of 1950s music.

That's right, the rock made music. It also gave news reports and weather forecasts.

I was 11 years old at the time and lived across the road from my best friend, a 19-year-old boy named James who had been totally paralyzed with polio. I was his legs and arms, and spent many summer afternoons sitting beside his layback wheelchair turning pages in his electronics magazines, and shooing away flies from his motionless face.

One lazy August afternoon, James said, "Let's build a crystal radio." And I've never been the same since hearing that statement.

He described the exact type of rock that I would need to find -- probably along the railroad tracks. I whizzed away on my bike toward the nearest tracks and soon returned with a cigar box full of crystal-lead rocks -- Galena, they were called.

I was then instructed to place the smallest one, about a half-inch square, in a tin catsup lid. Then, following James' every word, I cut a shotgun shell in two and emptied the lead bird-shot into a tin can and heated it until the lead started melting.

Holding the can with a pot holder, I poured the molten lead around the chunk of Galena, then stuck a copper wire into one side, allowing the lead to harden around the rock and the wire.

Then I took an old radio headphone and hooked one of its two wires to the buried-in-lead copper wire. The extreme other end of that wire was tied to a cold water pipe.

I then glued the catsup lid to a 1x4" board about 6" long and drove a nail next to the Galena, leaving the head sticking up a good quarter-inch. I took a five ft. piece of lamp cord and twisted the wire together, and wound about two inches of it around the nail head and bent the very end to where it touched the Galena rock. Then I was told to stick a straight pin through that twisted wire, and also to take the other headphone wire and attach it to the lamp cord, the other end of which had been attached to a window screen.

"Go ahead, listen to your radio," James said.

I placed the headphone over my right ear, and scratched the straight pin along the Galena rock until I heard KVOO radio booming in loud and clear.

It was a crude crystal radio, just like the ones which became so popular in the early 1920s after radio made its on-air debut.

By moving the pin, called a cat whisker, I found two different places where I could pick up radio stations -- KVOO and KAKC in Tulsa.

There was no electricity, no tubes or transistors, and certainly no chips or modules. It was just an old piece of Galena rock and a WWII surplus headphone, plus some wire.

I placed that radio on the window ledge next to my bed and listened every night to the sounds which emanated from KVOO and KAKC. When the night was quiet and the household sounds grew silent, I would drop the headphone in a one-gallon jar. I had to listen carefully, but each night I dozed off to sleep to the echoing sounds of nighttime radio ... thanks to an ingenious friend named James, and an afternoon project on his back porch.

Today's computer hacks with their talk of bytes, megs, ram upgrades, and C:\>. prompts, would do well to take a warm summer afternoon, find a chunk of Galena crystal, follow the "James" radio recipe, then find the shade of an oak tree and spend a couple hours listening to the sounds emerging from a gallon jar.

A good rock sounds pretty good, once it's tuned properly. But a little advice: Don't tell your friends what you're doing -- they'll throw you in the same category as a nutty editor. And any doctor will tell you there's no known cure for that predicament.

"Off the Cuff"

Joy is missed when children can't be old folks' friends

Each afternoon as my buddy Billy Wyckoff and I trudged home from school we would stop in front of Mr. George's house and talk with him. He predictably would give us an impromptu spelling test and chat with us about the world of baseball, then he'd always give us a stick of Beachnut gum.

We loved him, and we looked forward to our daily encounter with Mr. George who was a retired newspaper publisher.

I often wonder if today's children aren't being cheated from such friendships with old people, especially men.

With so many stories on TV about kinky men who lure children into their cars with promises of candy or gum, it has virtually eliminated the age-old game of visiting which old men enjoy playing with kids.

Now that I'm working on my second half-century of life, I find myself afraid to talk to small children, and never in a million years would touch one, let alone offer a stick of gum.

How sad that society has regressed to that point, because I've got lots of gum to give out, maybe some stories they'd like to hear, and I just know I'd be a good sidewalk master of a little spelling contest.

I am invigorated, encouraged and entertained by small children. When sitting in the local football stadium, I find myself pointing to the little toddlers who scamper along in front of their parents. I smile when I find out who they belong to, usually commenting that I remember when their parents were that size.

Although I have trouble remembering the names of half my adult friends, I can quickly recite most names of the wee ones.

It's because they're so energetic, cute and personable that I enjoy watching them. And I think it's a darn shame that I can't tweak one of their noses, or give one of them a pat, or reach in my pocket and offer every one of them a treat.

But I won't, because it's not proper. And I fully realize that.

I observed a man at the county courthouse today who, while standing in line to buy a car tag, struck up a conversation with a young mother holding a toddler-aged child. When it came time for her to write her check, it was necessary for her to put the child down.

"I'll keep an eye on her," the old gentleman said to the young woman. And he did just that. He never touched the child, but he stooped down and talked with the little girl who loved every minute of the episode.

Now, I wouldn't encourage any mother to let her child out of her sight for a minute, especially among strangers. But it was nice to see that the mother trusted the man to talk quietly, tease and play with the toddler, all at a watchful distance.

I watched the three of them walk down the courthouse hallway together, and they parted with smiles as they went their separate ways.

Old folks and children have so much in common, and it's too bad that men who make eyes at children are viewed with certain scorn.

Both sides are missing so much joy. I get proof of that when I re-tell the story of Mr. Frank George to my own children who never had the good fortune to know him.

I knew him so well because I grew up in a day when it was OK for old men to be good friends with little children.

"Off the Cuff"

Without Kansas in its big middle, America would fall off the earth

Here it is Jan. 28, so happy birthday, Kansas.

For a lass of 145, you're still in fabulous shape -- just starting to develop your sea legs, which is a pretty good trick for a prairie girl.

You've taken your share of undeserved jabs over the years, especially among those TV comedians who laugh at your flat chest, not realizing that your other terrain is fully blossomed, curvy and well endowed.

You've got a cute smile -- that wide stretch of prairie that sweeps from Sedan to Emporia to Abilene and north to the collar of your beautiful neck at the Nebraska state line.

Your giggle can be heard every time the wind blows that cool air in from the Colorado Rockies, and your sweet song drifts in and out while your children sleep in the quiet of dawn.

You've been jilted too often by ingrates who gained their wisdom from your mentoring, their stability from your warm embrace, their direction from your footprints, their strength from your traditions, and their very steps from your drum beat.

You're the center of America -- the prime piece of real estate in all the world. What you lack in mountains and oceans you make up in meandering rivers that bear the names of states: The Kansas, Arkansas and the wide Missouri.

Your skies seem bluer, wider and brighter than those in New York or Detroit, and the tall grasses on your prairies light up your eyes in deep green hues. Your days start early, your labor unending, and even your nights emit a certain glow as the stars of the heavens reflect from your waving wheat fields.

Your bashful passion wafts slowly yet lovingly as the mother nation sways to and fro. You gain few accolades for keeping this country on course, but everybody knows that without a solid, brave, unyielding, energized core, this nation would fall off the earth, and the big globe would wobble into the far off skies.

That makes you the belle of the universe, Lady Kansas. And, if ever anyone deserved a day of honor, it's the one whose name is like none other -- *Kansas*.

CHAPTER FOURTEEN

Everyone needs an angel

There is a hint of Bedford Falls in this little hometown.

The editor never compares himself directly to George Bailey from the movie, "It's a Wonderful Life!" but he admits to a certain fascination with the perennial holiday film.

The movie took place all in one fictional day, Dec. 24, 1945, the very day the Chronicle editor truly was born.

A couple years before "It's a Wonderful Life!" became a television favorite at Christmas-time, the editor ran across a video tape of the movie in a bin of old Hollywood classics at a local discount store.

Taking it home and viewing it was a life-changing experience for him, then only 40 years old. He wrote a column about it, challenging readers to look anew at their lives as something valuable, a link in the journey of humankind that would be missing had they never been born.

He closed the column with a sentence that brought a response, one that forever endeared him to the town he called home.

"I don't know whether my life would be missed or not, but I do know this, dear readers," the editor penned. "If you were missing from my life, it would be empty and sad. The joy found in our hometown would be diminished or perhaps quenched altogether. It is you whom we at the Chronicle envision as we sit down at our typewriters to write about our town and its people, activities, victories and defeats. Yes, you not only would be missed, but the vacuum of your absence would collapse the very walls around our beautiful little town."

That column brought a response from an anonymous writer, calling himself or herself "Clarence, ASC (Angel, Second Class).

In the first letter, Clarence tried to portray life without the Chronicle editor, noting that the town didn't need another bank, retail store or housing addition. It needed a poet laureate, and it had one.

It didn't stop there.

Each Christmas Eve, starting that year and continuing for the next decade, the editor would go to the post office and find a letter from his friend, Clarence the angel. They were literary keepsakes, quoting Thackery, Whittier and the psalmist David.

After the editor and his family had gone through a business failure, creating lots of public whispering, Clarence mused, "You have received of late some pointed and undeserved criticism. Never let it alter or diminish your purpose, for you 'are' the Chronicle, and Bedford Falls needs that blending of spirit and ink that weaves the common thread of belonging into the tender fabric of its soul.

"May the warm lamplight emanating from George Bailey's chambers burn long, burn bright ... far beyond this Christmas night.

"Happy birthday, George, and Merry Christmas!

Your friend, Clarence."

They stopped arriving in about 1997, and the editor never knew who wrote them. But they remain in a secret place within his office where they can be retrieved any time discouragement sets in, or life takes a bounce out of the fairway and into the deep rough.

His office wall is decorated with all kinds of memorabilia, but none so meaningful as a show bill from the original movie which co-starred Jimmy Stewart and Donna Reed. Clarence is never far from the editor's view.

The Chronicle editor's family tries, to this day, to guess who Clarence might have been, always wondering if he or she might still be out there somewhere.

It is a discussion the editor refuses to join.

He just assumes every person he meets on the street is Clarence. That way, maybe he will act the way anyone would want to act in the presence of an angel.

And when he hits a winner in life, he invariably looks to the skies, winks, and quietly says, "Atta boy, Clarence."

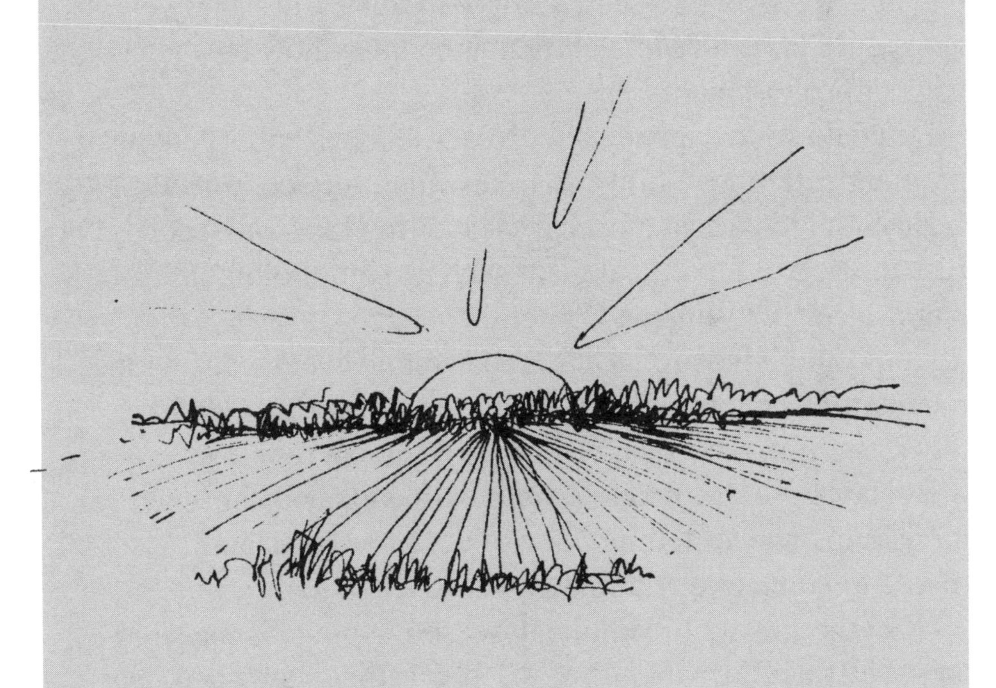

"Off the Cuff"

The Christmas baby

At our house, nothing stops us in our tracks faster than a TV commercial featuring a little baby.

You know the ones -- babies are used to sell everything from tires to talcum powder, and I can understand why: Everybody finds a baby to be irresistible. So, whether I'm seeking a ball game to watch on TV, or my wife is searching for her favorite sitcom, or our teenaged daughter browses the shelf of video movies, we all three come together anytime a baby commercial hits the air.

I can't speak for the Creator of the Universe who found it in his infinite wisdom to send a savior to this earth 2,000 years ago. But I have a deep feeling that he knew how best to capture the hearts of all mankind.

He could have zapped us with obedient and robot-like hearts, programmed to love him and follow his every command.

He could have sent a military leader the likes of Napoleon or Eisenhower, or a political giant such as King Solomon, Abraham Lincoln or Winston Churchill.

God could have produced a cataclysmic event, causing the mountains to move and the oceans to swell. He could have sent the Messiah in a hurricane, tornado or atop a rainbow.

But he chose the direct route to our hearts. He chose a tiny baby as his way of telling the world, "I love you, and I want all of you to come live with me in Heaven."

In all the songs of the holiday season, none tells the story so sweetly as *Away in a Manger.* It was that way when Jesus Christ was born -- shepherds came from the hills; kings came from the Orient; and they converged on a tiny town not unlike the small villages and towns of southeast Kansas.

God didn't choose Rome or Athens as the birthplace of our Lord. He didn't inspire leading scholars and religious authors to write about the event. And he didn't look to royalty to be Jesus' earthly parents.

In fact, the whole life of Christ was uncommonly common. He was a carpenter's son, and his mother a teenager. As far as we know, he never owned a thing. He walked and talked with the people of his homeland, healing their ills, telling of his father's great love for them, and promising eternal life to anyone willing to believe in his teachings and follow his commands.

Today, people from around the world still observe his birthday, follow his teachings, and cling to his promises. That's how great he was. And is. And always will be.

We often find ourselves seeking happiness in the form of money, possessions, events and popularity, and ultimately end our lives finding all to be vanity. That is, unless we visit the manger in Bethlehem and cast our eyes upon the One who came to show us the way to true love and happiness.

Everybody loves a baby. But in this case, it was the baby who loved us first. And, quite honestly, dear reader, I can't fathom living one day without knowing Him.

Merry Christmas, everyone, every day of the year!

"Off the Cuff"

My favorite place

My favorite place is not a cottage by the seaside nor a chateau in the alps with a lovely mountain view.

It is not a forest of pines nor the rolling hills of a tallgrass prairie.

This place requires no expense to keep it beautiful, no reservation to stay there, no rules to follow once you arrive.

My favorite place lures the rich and poor, young and old, ill or well.

Above it you will find no sign of lighted letters, no sounds to make you dance, no aroma to pique your senses.

It is a simple place. One where you will find solace yet warmth, comfort yet excitement, smiles yet tears.

It is not a puzzle, rather it is a prescription for peace, for my favorite place is *a soft shoulder.*

A soft shoulder awaits those who need love, comfort, assurance and peace.

Children learn from birth the security found on a soft shoulder and it stays with them through their youth and finally into their teenage years when a new face finds the path to this secret garden.

It will be there that love spawns, conflicts resolve and hurtful words vanish.

Soldiers seek the soft shoulder of a friend as they lay dying on the battlefield.

Girlfriends find it when he can't find the proper words.

And folks in the wintertime of their lives covet a soft shoulder where they can reflect, relax and finally ... rest.

It's my favorite place in all the world.

The soft shoulder.

"Off the Cuff"

Last night's pillow and the next morning's light

I try to leave all of yesterday's troubles, sins and conflicts on my pillow, and just before falling asleep each night, I pray for that wonderful forgiveness that only the grace of God can bring.

Then, I sleep well.

No alarm clock is needed by a country editor who has seven papers to get to press by Wednesday. My feet hit the ground with a bounce of energy, and my "list of things to do" starts mulling around in my mind before I enjoy that first cup of coffee.

Still, the greatest gift at this early hour is the peace with which I begin each day -- thanking Him for taking last night's burdens and placing them in that span called East from West. I get to start all over again every day.

I'm about as imperfect as any man the good Lord ever created. I think the wrong thoughts, make impulsive decisions, stir unneeded emotions, and procrastinate doing the most important things in life. And I sin.

That's why, during those wee hours of the morning, I find myself a little nervous, fully confident that the sun will, indeed, come up, but realizing that God might someday make yesterday the last day I'll ever see.

I quickly shower, shave and dress. I then head out the door and drive toward my office, and depending on what time of year it is, I get to witness a beautiful sunrise as I drive. What a glorious vista I am allowed to see each day, and how fortunate I am to visit His divine gallery of heavenly art.

When I was little, my dad would get up early, go to the barn, place one boot on the bottom rung of the white fence, lean gently forward, and watch as the eastern horizon brightened with reddish light. He then would finish his chores and whistle his favorite tune as he peacefully started another day.

I'm not aware of my dad's imperfections in life, but I'm sure he had some. He surely must have found the same solace in daily forgiveness that I find with morning's light.

Today's world would be so much better if everyone looked to the first light of day as their signal that God is alive, well and craving a chance to embrace, heal and forgive. It is available to all those who look His way, acknowledge and follow Him.

The prayer that I inevitably whisper is a humble one. I dare not say it aloud, for my life is cluttered with thoughts that only my Lord would understand. It is after that session, however brief, that I can face another day, with all my yesterdays blotted out, and a clean sheet of parchment ready to start my new day's list.

And tonight it too shall disappear on my pillow.

Lighting the way ...

Little birds floating high above,
can you see me here below?

My sail glows in the sunset,
waves bounce me to and fro.

The jagged rocks that line the shore
make me tremble at their sight.

But that ivory covered lighthouse
keeps beaming, oh, so bright.

So far from shore, I sometimes drift,
yet I'm safe and always sure.

I'm nestled between your heavens,
and the beacon that burns so pure.

Come down, little birds,
when you need a restful ride.

Perch on my sailboat's bow,
sleep gently at my side.

Shine, you big beacon,
light my course that I may see ...

The way back home at this day's end
and tomorrow again, I'll sail your sea.

"Off the Cuff"

Making tracks together

Railroad trestles have always fascinated me.

There is something enamoring about walking on a rail across a small bridge, teetering along, one foot in front of the other, always fearing that inevitable fall to the perils below.

Then one sees another rail walker beside him on the other track, sharing all the fun, heading in the same direction but also sensing the risk of that outside fall. Only inside the tracks can one be assured of safety.

Then it occurs to them both. Lean to the middle just a little, reach out and take the other's hand and walk the rails together toward the other side. There is no way to fall outside the rails when you've got a friend to walk beside you and offer such strength and balance.

Life is a lot like those steel rails. We know where we're going and we know the lines. Outside, there is pain, despair, tragedy. Inside, even though we dizzily bounce from side to side, we find safety, assurance and destiny.

Walk with me, friend.

And lean in, ever so gently.

I'll be there for you.

"Off the Cuff"

The power of finding the soft side

I admit to having a rosy outlook on life. It is a mentality that has cost me a lot of money during this lifetime and has caused more than one skirmish with my wife, employees and other family members who sometimes call me "soft."

"You let people walk all over you," they tell me.

I plead guilty and I'm not necessarily proud that I've gained that reputation.

Still, when I read the words of Jesus -- the ones in red letters -- I see a man whom I want to emulate. I see a man of compassion. Wisdom, Truth. Love. Finesse. I also see a man who walked among us wearing a mantle of strength unparalleled by any lineman who ever banged heads with a fellow 300-pounder on the opposing side.

So, it's not an either/or man that I try to be.

The Jesus I know and love was, and is, one with a soft side to him. He observed people and their burdens. He looked into their eyes and read their true thoughts. He noticed those special little episodes as he walked along his pathway, like the fellow named Zachius who climbed a tree just to get a glimpse of his savior.

I am touched by the stark fear that Jesus sensed in the hearts of his apostles while they were caught in a small boat during a storm. I remember the downtrodden woman at the well who never dreamed she might again have possibilities for a full, enriched life. But after her encounter with Jesus, she found new tomorrows that were full of hope.

As an editor, I am often confronted by people who, for some reason, think I want to hotly debate current events and the issues surrounding them. When I occasionally get wise enough to apply the WWJD rule, I allow them to vent their views and wear down their frustrations. It is then that I sometimes get an opportunity to say something encouraging, uplifting or maybe even inspirational. Inevitably, both the talker and the listener end up as winners.

I have a friend who, 30 years ago, was my hometown's stellar football player. Had it not been for a knee injury during his senior year, he would have played major college football. Today, he is an avid outdoorsman and a genius of designing and building "things." Give him a scrap of metal or a pile of wood and he will craft something useful of it.

But his close friends also know he has a delicate touch with decorating an angel food cake. He has a wonderfully soft side to him.

Another friend is a former PRCA rodeo performer and now teaches elementary school in my hometown. He can chew, spit, ride bulls and train horses for rodeo cowboys.

Tough guy.

I've also noticed that he keeps dozens of poetry books on his bookshelf and he often shares his favorite Shakespearian sonnets with his sixth grade students.

Big man. Big heart. Soft man. Bigger man in my eyes.

We all must decide our purpose in life and the way we want to think, act and react. I have no idea how my friends look at my crazy outlook on life, but *I know in Whom I have believed, and am persuaded that He is able to keep me against His promises made unto that day.*

Sometimes that requires a "game face." Hopefully, the majority of my time on this earth is being spent with the other face, the one that is perceived as being "soft" in my role as a community publisher.

One day soon, in the heavens, I will face the One who has always been my mentor. On that day, I pray that he will be wearing his soft face, not the tough one, and that He will welcome me into His big, compassionate arms --- undeserving, ill-prepared and scared that I will be.

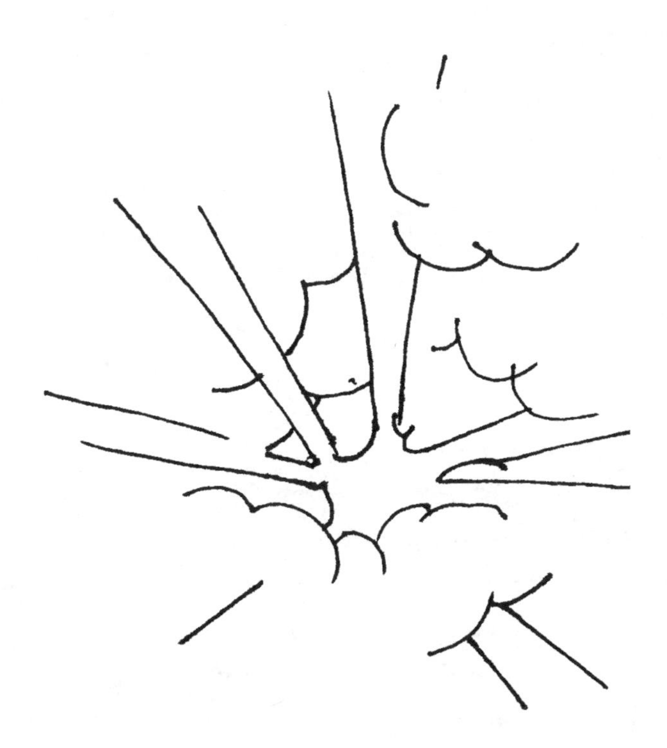

EPILOGUE

The front door is where most light comes pouring in

Sometimes the editor wonders why a door was ever placed at the front of a country newspaper office.

That door is seldom locked.

So many times, the Chronicle editor has walked home for supper and never made it back to the office, more than likely diverted by someone who wanted him to take a picture or give him a news story.

As a result, the telephone in his bedroom often has rung in the middle of the night with a police dispatcher dryly saying, “You need to meet Elmer at your office. You forgot to lock your door again.”

Elmer was the night watchman who rattled doors twice a night.

But there were times when the officer had more pressing matters than checking doors, so the Chronicle office remained unlocked, with lights glowing, throughout the night.

That’s where the editor got the idea for *“Light On Main Street,”* because as he approached that office at 2 in the morning, it seemed to illuminate the entire avenue. Long after the clothing store had shut off its display windows and long after the neon light above the drugstore had dimmed to darkness, there remained a light in the front office of the hometown Chronicle.

He was always afraid to say much about it, fearing that

folks might think the editor was making himself out to be some kind of a beacon.

Nothing like that.

But there were lights in that little town and there still are today, some of them bright, some barely visible. They come from the eyes of children and the smiles of elderly friends who intervene in the life of the hometown editor every day.

Lights of hope come in the form of handwritten notes sent in with subscription renewals. "We couldn't live without our little Chronicle," they will say.

They come from pastors who serve the town so humbly, so willingly, so selflessly. These men and women of God never realize how many times they inspired a column or editorial in the newspaper that seemed to lift the spirits of these small-town residents.

The light on Main Street is not a lighthouse nor a brilliant strobe. It emanates from every house in town, every heart that beats, every person who falls down and gets up again, every high school team that loses 10 football games in a season and still lifts the coach to their shoulders.

Light on the editor's Main Street bounces into that open front door, brightens every corner, encourages a family that works late on deadline and returns to the street through the columns of the Chronicle.

It's been that way for over 120 years in this hometown. And an admittedly naive editor believes the shimmering lights that he has seen, and hopefully reflected, in his lifetime will illuminate the town for another hundred years.

The "thud" of the hometown Chronicle hitting the doorstep is a sound nobody should miss.

No longer will you need the sun or moon
to give you light, for the Lord your God will be
your everlasting light, and He will be your glory.

Isaiah 60:19

- 30 -

Rudy Taylor